SUPER CHARGE YOUR SPECTRUM

SUPER CHARGE YOUR SPECTRUM

DAVID WEBB

MELBOURNE HOUSE PUBLISHERS

Published in the United Kingdom by:
Melbourne House (Publishers) Ltd.,
Church Yard,
Tring, Hertfordshire HP23 5LU,
ISBN 0 - 86161 - 112 - 8

Published in Australia by:
Melbourne House (Australia) Pty. Ltd.,
Suite 4, 75 Palmerston Crescent,
South Melbourne, Victoria, 3205,

Published in the United States of America by:
Melbourne House Software Inc.,
347 Reedwood Drive,
Nashville TN 37217.

Printed in Hong Kong by Colorcraft Ltd.

D C B A 9 8 7 6 5 4 3 2 1

SPECIAL NOTE

The programs and routines in this book represent a very unusual willingness on the part of a machine language programmer to disclose exactly how his routines are written.

David Webb has done so from a desire to help other programmers develop their own programs and to teach machine language programming by example. They are intended to be used as a tool for learning and for use in your own personal programs.

However, it is not the intention that these routines be used in any commercially produced programs, and we would like you to note that these programs and routines are covered by the laws of copyright.

After reading and working through this book, I am sure you will agree that David Webb has produced a work that will be of great assistance to Spectrum programmers everywhere.

Best regards,

Alfred Milgrom
Publisher

CONTENTS

Routines to improve BASIC commands

Utility routines

Enhancing your programs

APPENDICES

PREFACE

Any reader who has purchased one of the multitude of
machine-coded arcade games available for the ZX Spectrum will
appreciate the vast difference in speed and power between
machine language and BASIC programs. Until now the only way
for a BASIC Programmer to achieve this power has been to
'buckle down' to the ominous task of actually learning to
"speak the lingo".

In this book I aim to make machine code techniques freely
available to the BASIC programmer without him or her needing to
worry about how they work. Each of the routines is a small,
self-contained block of machine code with full instructions on
how to use it. In the first two chapters I provide all the
information, programs and simple techniques you'll need to use
the rest of the book. No knowledge of machine code is
necessary, but for the reader who has such knowledge I have
included a fully commented assembly mnemonic listing for each
routine.

In response to the many requests I have seen for a full list of
useful POKES and system variables on the ZX Spectrum, I have
included the appropriate information in this book. Also
included are machine language solutions to the problem of
recognising graphic characters with the SCREEN$ function, and
to that of using the erroneous PAUSE command.

I would like to extend my thanks to the following people:
     - Mum and Dad, for seventeen years of unbelievable
tolerance.

- Alfred Milgrom, my publisher, for his support and
encouragement.
- My teachers at Woking 6th form College, for ignoring the
slight absence of homework on the five A-levels and two
S-levels for which I was studying while writing this book.

DAVID M. WEBB
WOKING, ENGLAND
JULY 1983

GETTING STARTED

CHAPTER 1
USING THE ROUTINES:- ALL YOU NEED TO KNOW

Unless you are fluent in machine code and have your own machine
code monitor program, you will need to read this chapter and
the next which contain all the information and programs
necessary to use the routines in the rest of the book.

First let me explain a few simple ideas. Your computer probably
has either 16K or 48K of Random Access Memory (RAM) in it,
together with a 16K Read Only Memory (ROM) which houses the
large machine language program that makes the Spectrum work in
BASIC. The 'K' stands for 'Kilobyte', and one may be forgiven
for equating this to 1000 bytes. In actual fact, because of the
way computers count in binary (i.e. multiples of 1, 2, 4, 8...)
'Kilo-' means 2^{10} or 1024, so each 'K' of memory contains 1024
bytes. Each byte is like my bank account; it can store a whole
number between 0 and 255. Now the computer needs to know where
each of these numbers is stored, so it gives each byte a unique
number which we call an ADDRESS (like a bank account no.).

The commands 'PEEK' and 'POKE' simply 'find out' and 'change'
what is stored at a specified address, so entering the command:

          PRINT PEEK 0

tells us what number is stored at the first address in the ROM
(in the case of the Spectrum, 243).

The ZX-Spectrum has what is known as an eight-bit
microprocessor, the Z-80A. This is the real 'brain' of the
computer, the part which obeys all the machine language

instructions in the ROM and RAM. Microprocessors do not work in
BASIC. (BASIC is what is known as a 'high-level' language). It
is easy for we mortals to write programs in BASIC, but in order
for the microprocessor to understand our commands they have to
be "translated" into a machine language program. The BASIC
INTERPRETER breaks down the BASIC into a set of 'low-level'
machine language instructions which can then be executed by the
Z-80A.

All of this 'interpretation' takes time, a great deal in fact,
which is why by writing out programs directly in machine
language we can achieve an average speed increase in the order
of 100 times.

In order to fetch data and instructions from the memory, the
microprocessor must send the address of the required byte along
what is known as the ADDRESS BUS. There are only 16 lines or
'seats' on this bus, and so the address can only be two Bytes
long. (Eight bits per byte, one line per bit and each bit set
to 1 or 0.)

The highest number that we can represent in two bytes is 65535,
produced by filling both bytes with the 255 maximum. We let one
byte count the 'units' (the LO byte of the address) and the
other byte count the multiples of 256 (the HI byte). So

$$(255 \times 256) + 255 = 65535$$
$$\text{HI} \qquad\qquad \text{LO}$$

The lowest number we can represent is, of course, zero, when
both the hi and lo byte are zero. The concept of 'hi' and 'lo'
bytes can be analogised to 'tens' and 'units' when we count in
normal decimal arithmetic. We say then that

$$27 = (2 \times 10) \qquad + 7$$
$$\text{HI byte} \qquad \text{LO byte}$$

Now we can see that the maximum number of memory addresses that
the Z-80A with its 16-bit address bus can access is 65536. On
the Spectrum, addresses 0 to 16383 (the first 16K) are taken up
by the ROM. 16K of RAM follows on from address 16384 to 32767,
the first 6.75K of which is used up for screen memory. Finally,
if you have a 48K machine, the last 32K of addresses up to
65535 are consumed by the extra RAM.

This allocation of addresses can be shown with a MEMORY MAP.
Here is a memory map showing the areas we are chiefly concerned
with (a more complete memory map can be found on page 165 of
the official manual).

ROM	Text and Graphics RAM	Colour RAM	Printer Buffer	System Variables etc.	BASIC Program + Variables	Spare	User Definable Graphics

STKEND →   UDG (end of RAM)

16384   22528   23296   23552   PROG   RAMTOP   P RAM

16K   6K   ¾K   ¼K   168 Bytes

4

As you can see, between the BASIC area and the only thing normally in 'high memory', the user-definable graphics, is whatever spare memory you may have. Normally this is decreased by increasing the length of your program and/or producing larger BASIC variables (letting the program 'grow upwards' in memory). You can, however use up this spare memory by lowering the pointer shown as RAMTOP, beyond which no BASIC program is allowed to expand (the TOP of BASIC RAM). This operation has the effect of reserving and protecting the memory space between RAMTOP and UDG, which is another pointer indicating the start of the user graphics.

The values of these pointers are stored in the 'system variables' area. RAMTOP can be found by the command

PRINT PEEK 23730 + 256 * PEEK 23731

and will be 32599 on a 16K Spectrum or 65367 on a 48K machine at power-up.

UDG can be found with

PRINT PEEK 23675 + 256 * PEEK 23676

but far more easily with the command

PRINT USR "a"

Since this returns the address of the first user-defined character, "graphic a" which is naturally enough at the start of the user-definable graphics area. The value of UDG will be 32600 or 65368 at power-up, thereby showing that there is normally no space between RAMTOP and UDG.

To alter the value of RAMTOP we simply use the command CLEAR n, where n is the new address for RAMTOP.

When we have lowered RAMTOP with a CLEAR command then an area of memory between RAMTOP and UDG has been reserved, and it is in this space that we usually put machine code. Everything that is stored above RAMTOP is completely unaffected by anything we do in BASIC other than a POKE, which alters the contents of a specified address, including a NEW command. This means that we can store machine-code utility routines such as a 'renumber' program, above RAMTOP and never have to worry about losing them when we LOAD up a different program or do a NEW.

Machine Code in its raw form is simply a collection of numbers that the microprocessor interprets as instructions and obeys accordingly. We choose to represent these numbers in a form known as HEXADECIMAL, or base 16 (HEX for six, DEC for ten). We use the symbols 0 to 9 and A to F (for ten to fifteen), and with two hex. digits we can represent the numbers 0 to 255, or 00 to FF in hex.

All of the machine code routines in this book have a HEX
LISTING; it is this column of hex numbers which should be typed
into the computer. To make life easier we use a MONITOR program
which supervises the entry of machine code and lets you do
things like list entered code, save it, alter it and load it
back from tape.

Below you will find a monitor program which I have called
HEXAID. It will enable you to type in hex routines and
manipulate them to your heart's content. It may seem a little
long, but it is essential to the rest of the book. I will
explain how to use it when you have typed it in!

```
100 REM Hexaid (c) David M. Web
b 1982
110 POKE 23658,8: CLS : GO SUB
870: PRINT '"Menu:"
120 PRINT '"[1]:WRITE a new rou
tine"
130 PRINT '"[2]:ALTER a routine
"
140 PRINT '"[3]:LIST Hex. code"
150 PRINT '"[4]:SAVE a routine"
160 PRINT '"[5]:LOAD a routine"
170 PRINT '"[6]:STOP this progr
am"
180 PRINT '"[7]:CLEAR the machi
ne code area"
190 PRINT #0;AT  1,0;"Please pr
ess appropriate key."
200  IF INKEY$<>"" THEN  GO TO
200
210 LET g$=INKEY$: IF g$="" OR
g$<"1" OR g$>"7" THEN  GO TO 210
220 IF g$="6" THEN  STOP
230 CLS : GO SUB 870: GO SUB 93
0
250 GO TO (270 AND G$="1")+(460
 AND G$="2")+(500 AND G$="3")+(5
90 AND G$="4")+(710 AND G$="5")+
(820 AND G$="7")
260 REM WRITE a new routine
270 INPUT "Length of routine:";
LINE a$: GO SUB M
280 CLEAR RAMTOP-VAL  a$: GO SU
B 870: GO SUB 930:
290 LET d=RAMTOP+1
300 LET a$=""
310 IF a$="" THEN  INPUT "Enter
hex. code.";a$
320 GO SUB M
330 IF LEN a$/2<>INT (LEN a$/2)
THEN  PRINT "Incorrect entry";:
GO TO 300
```

6

```
 350 LET C=0: FOR f=1  TO  16 ST
EP 15
 360 LET a=CODE a$(1+(F=1))
 370 IF a<48 OR a>70 OR a>57 AND
 a<65 THEN  PRINT "Incorrect ent
ry";: GO TO 300
 380 LET c=c+f*((a<58)*(a-48)+(a
>64 AND a<71)*(a-55)): NEXT f
 400 POKE d,c: LET d=d+1
 410 PRINT a$( TO 2);"  ";
 420 LET a$=a$(3 TO )
 430 IF d=USR "a" THEN  PRINT "W
arning:you are now in user"'"gra
phic area!": GO TO 300

 440 GO TO 310
 450 REM ALTER a routine
 460 PRINT "Alter from address:"
;: INPUT  LINE a$: GO SUB M
 470 LET d=VAL a$: PRINT d
 480 GO TO 300
 490 REM LIST hex code
 500 LET b$="0123456789ABCDEF"
 510 PRINT '"list address:";: IN
PUT  LINE a$: GO SUB M: LET d=VA
L a$
 520 PRINT AT 4,22;"press";AT 7,
0;
 530 LET a=INT (PEEK d/16): LET
b=PEEK d-16*A
 540 PRINT d;TAB 7;b$(a+1);b$(b+
1)
 550 LET d=d+1
 560 IF INKEY$="M" THEN  RUN
 570 GO TO 530
 580 REM SAVE a routine
 590 PRINT '"save from address:"
;: INPUT  LINE a$: GO SUB M: LET
 a=VAL a$: PRINT a
 600 PRINT '"Length of routine:"
;: INPUT  LINE a$: GO SUB M: PRI
NT VAL A$
 610 PRINT '"Name of routine:";:
 INPUT n$: PRINT n$

 620 SAVE n$CODE a,VAL a$
 630 PRINT '"Do you wish to veri
fy (Y\N)?";
 640 PAUSE 0: LET v$=INKEY$: PRI
NT v$
 650 IF v$<>"Y" THEN  RUN
 660 PRINT '"Rewind and press ""
PLAY."""
 670 VERIFY n$CODE
 680 PRINT '"O.K.": PAUSE 50: RU
N
```

```
 700 REM LOAD a routine
 710 PRINT '"Shall I make extra
room in the"'"machine code area
(Y/N)?"
 720 IF INKEY$<>"" THEN  GO TO 7
20
 730 LET a$=INKEY$: IF a$="" THE
N  GO TO 730
 750 GO SUB M: IF a$<>"Y" THEN
GO TO 770
 760 INPUT "How many bytes?"; LI
NE a$: GO SUB M: CLEAR RAMTOP-VA
L a$: GO SUB 870: GO SUB 930

 770 PRINT '"Load to address:";:
INPUT  LINE a$: GO SUB M: PRINT
a$
 780 PRINT '"Routine name:";: IN
PUT n$: PRINT n$
 790 PRINT '"Press ""PLAY"" on t
ape."
 800 LOAD n$CODE VAL a$: GO TO 6
80
 810 REM  CLEAR the machine code
 area
 820 PRINT '"Are you sure (Y/N)?
"
 830 IF INKEY$<>"" THEN  GO TO 8
30
 840 LET a$=INKEY$: IF a$="" THE
N  GO TO 840
 850 IF a$<>"Y" THEN  RUN
 860 CLEAR USR "A"-1: RUN
 870 REM SETUP
 880 LET RAMTOP=PEEK 23730+256*P
EEK 23731
 900 PRINT "Start of M.C. area="
;RAMTOP+1
 910 PRINT '"Length of M.C. area
=";USR "A"-RAMTOP-1;" bytes."
 920 LET M=940: RETURN
 930 PRINT '"To return to the me
nu,enter ""M""."; RETURN
 940 IF a$="M" THEN  RUN
 950 RETURN
```

You are advised to save HEXAID before you go any further.

Hexaid works with the CAPS LOCK on: be careful not to go into
lower case while you are running it. When the program is RUN it
presents you with a menu of seven options. The first and most
important is 'Write a new routine'. On selecting this you are
asked to enter the length of the routine. This is the number of
bytes of code in the 'HEX' column in each routine's listing,
and is always found at the top right-hand corner of the
listing.

When you INPUT the length the program automatically moves down
RAMTOP with a CLEAR command (line 280) and thereby makes
exactly enough space in the machine code area for the routine.
(Between RAMTOP & UDG) You are then asked to "enter hex code".
In response to this you simply read off the 'HEX' column of the
routine and enter it into the program as many bytes at a time
as you like, working across and down the column.

When you enter the length of the routine, the 'start of M.C.
Area', printed at the top of the screen always decreases by the
length of the routine. Make sure that you always note down this
new value, as this is the START ADDRESS or "address of the
first byte" of your routine, and will be used with the USR
function later on.

When you have finished entering all the hex code for a routine,
it is wise to check the printout on the screen against the
listing in the book. The slightest error, a 3 entered instead
of an 8 or an 8 instead of a B can change the entire meaning of
an instruction and cause the computer to 'crash'. This doesn't
do any permanent damage to your computer, if it happens, just
'reset' and start again.

You can list the routine at any time by returning to the menu,
choosing option 3; 'list hex code' and entering the start
address. This will induce a column of hex code with its
locations to appear on the screen.

If you find that you have made an error in the hex. code then
note down the address of the 'rogue' byte(s) from the 'list'
option, return to the menu (by pressing 'm') and choose option
2: 'Alter a routine'.

Here again you are asked to input the address of the rogue
byte(s) and then the hex code, to which you should reply with
the corrected byte(s).

When you are satisfied that the code is correct, select option
4 in order to SAVE the routine to tape. You are asked
successively for the start address, the length and the name of
the routine; the latter should, as usual, not be longer than
ten characters. The essential part of this section is the SAVE
... CODE command in line 620. What this does is to save a
specified number of bytes of machine code from a specified
start address. You could, in fact, perform exactly the same
operation by entering, in immediate mode:

SAVE "(routine name)" CODE (start address), (routine length).

Hexaid then gives you the option of VERIFYING, again based on
the simple command in line 670; equivalent to

          VERIFY "(routine name)" CODE   –

9

Note that if the start address and routine length have not been altered then they need not be specified in the VERIFY command.

Option 5: "load a routine" lets you LOAD back a routine from tape. It is particularly useful if you have found that a routine you were using crashed the machine, as this usually means that you made a mistake in the hex. code and will need to LOAD it back, in order to detect the 'bug'.

On choosing the option you are asked if you want to make extra room in the machine code area. If the length of the M.C. area is longer than or equal to your routine and you don't mind overwriting part of what is already in that area then the answer is "no". If, however, the M.C. area is shorter than your routine or you don't want to alter what is already there then you do want to expand the M.C. area (answer Y).

If the answer was 'Y' then you must input the number of bytes by which the M.C. area is to be lengthened. This is usually equal to the length of the routine. The program will lower RAMTOP to the required address (1 less than the "start of M.C. area").

Finally you are asked "Load to address:" to which you will probably reply with the start of the M.C. area, as displayed at the top of the screen.

The essential part of this section is line 800, which can be emulated with the direct command

            LOAD "(routine name)" CODE (start address)

You can make room for and load machine code from within your own programs by 'tagging on' a few simple lines:

            9900 LET RAMTOP = PEEK 23730 + 256*PEEK 23731
            9910 RETURN
            9920 GOSUB 9900 : CLEAR RAMTOP - (routine
                              length)
            9930 GOSUB 9900 : LOAD "(routine name)" CODE
                              RAMTOP+1
            9940 RUN

Line 9920 makes room; line 9930 loads. The start address of the routine will now be RAMTOP + 1.

The last two options in Hexaid are option 6: "stop the program" and option 7: "clear the machine code area". The latter should be used with great care, as it will reset RAMTOP to its original position, immediately below the user graphics area, thereby deleting all of the machine code present. For this reason I have incorporated line 820; "are you sure?". So if you accidentally hit the 7 key all will not be lost. The essential line is 860, which CLEARS RAMTOP to USR "a" (UDG) minus one.

USING THE ROUTINES

All of the routines in this book have specific instructions
with them that will enable you to use them to the full, so I
will only talk in general terms here.

Many of the longer routines require some data in order to work,
such as the corners of a rectangle for 'scrolling' routines or
the first line number in a 'renumber' routine. This is either
POKEd into the routine, or, more usually, into the PRINTER
BUFFER, which is 256 bytes long from address 23296. As you
might imagine, the printer also uses this memory, so if you use
the printer while using the routines then any data will be lost
and must be POKEd in again before CALLING the routine.

To CALL a routine means to execute it, and this is always done
with the USR function, which is usually incorporated in a
RAMDOMIZE or LET statement, thus:

        RANDOMIZE USR (start address)
or   LET L = USR   (start address)

USING HEXAID: A WORKING EXAMPLE

In order for you to practice using the Hexaid program and the
techniques I have taught you to date, here is a short routine
for you to enter.

```
HEX.            ;MYSTERY ROUTINE! LENGTH: 39 BYTES
3E02        MYSTERY LD      A,2
CD0116          CALL    1601H
3E12            LD      A,12H
D7              RST     10H
3E01            LD      A,1
D7              RST     10H
3E57            LD      A,57H
D7              RST     10H
3E45            LD      A,45H
D7              RST     10H
3E4C            LD      A,4CH
D7              RST     10H
3E4C            LD      A,4CH
D7              RST     10H
3E20            LD      A,20H
D7              RST     10H
3E44            LD      A,44H
D7              RST     10H
3E4F            LD      A,4FH
D7              RST     10H
3E4E            LD      A,4EH
D7              RST     10H
3E45            LD      A,45H
D7              RST     10H
C9              RET
                END
```

Using option one of Hexaid, the "length of routine" will be 39 bytes. If the M.C. area was previously of zero length, then its length should now be 39 bytes and the start address of the routine and the M.C. area should be 32561 (16K) or 65329 (48K).

When you have SAVEd the routine using option four, you are ready to call the routine with

      RANDOMIZE USR 32561 (16K)
or   RANDOMIZE USR 65329 (48K)
or   RANDOMIZE USR (start address), if your start address is different to the ones above. If you have done all this successfully, a brief message will appear on the screen. If not, then load the routine with option five and use options three and two to correct the code.

CHAPTER 2
BUILDING A DEDICATED TOOLKIT FROM A LIBRARY OF ROUTINES

To prevent yourself having to type in the same routines with Hexaid every time you want to use them for a different BASIC program, it is obviously a good idea to build up a 'library' of your favourite routines, adding to it with Hexaid each time you use a new routine. Then whenever you start writing a new program you can just select the routines that you think you will need and put them together in one 'Dedicated Toolkit', (a block of routines that has been purpose-designed for one particular program).

To help you to do that, I have written a program that reads the 'headers' in front of each routine on tape and then presents you with a 'catalogue' of all the routines, along with the addresses that they were saved from and their lengths. After each routine has been 'read' you have the option of stopping the catalogue and loading up any of the previous routines under program control or stopping the program altogether. In this way you can scan through the tape, picking up the routines that you want until you have a complete dedicated toolkit.

Before I go any further I'll let you have the listing. It's quite a long one, but it will save you a great deal of time in the long run (you can, of course, omit all the REMs).

```
  10 REM ROUTINE SELECTOR
  20 REM © DAVID M. WEBB,1983
  30 REM WARNING ONLY RUN THIS O
NCE. USE GOTO 100 THEREAFTER TO
  RE-ENTER PROGRAM
```

```
40 POKE 23658,8: REM   PROGRAM
WILL ONLY WORK WHILE CAPS LOCK I
S ON
   50 REM CREATE M.C. AREA AND IN
ITIALIZE POINTERS
   60 GO SUB 420 : CLEAR RT-3000:
GO SUB 420: LET MC=RT+3001: LET
MCL=0: LET N=MCL: LET NB=MCL
   70 GO SUB 310: LET F=50: DIM A
$(F,10): DIM B$(F,10): DIM S(F):
DIM T(F): DIM L(F): DIM M(F): R
EM F=NO. OF FILES
   80 REM A$,B$ HOLD NAMES,(S),(T
) HOLD START ADDRESSES,(L),(M)HO
LD LENGTHS.
   90 REM USE"GOTO100" TO REPRINT
CATALOG
   100 PRINT TAB 8; INVERSE 1;"ROU
TINE CATALOG."'': PRINT " FILENA
ME";TAB 12;"FROM ADDRESS";TAB 26
;"LENGTH"
   110 FOR A=1 TO N: GO SUB 410: N
EXT A: REM PRINT CATALOG
   120 GO SUB 450: GO SUB 350
   130 LET N=N+1: LET A$(N)=N$: LE
T S(N)=S: LET L(N)=L
   140 LET A=N: GO SUB 410
   150 INPUT "": PRINT #0;"PRESS S
NOW TO STOP CATALOG."
   160 FOR A=0 TO 400: IF INKEY$="
S" THEN  GO TO 180
   170 NEXT A: INPUT "": GO TO 120
   180 INPUT "LOAD A ROUTINE OR ST
OP PROGRAM (L/S)?";X$
   190 IF X$(1)="S" THEN  STOP
   200 POKE 23658,0: INPUT "PROUTI
NE NAME?";X$: POKE 23658,8
   210 LET X$=X$+"          "( TO
10-LEN X$): REM 10 SPACES
   220 FOR A=1 TO N: IF X$=A$(A) T
HEN  GO TO 240
   230 NEXT A: PRINT "NOT FOUND:-P
LEASE RETYPE": BEEP .25,10: GO T
O 200
   240 PRINT : GO SUB 410: GO SUB
430
   250 PRINT "OPTIONS:"''"[1] STAND
ARD LOAD INTO M.C. AREA[2] LOAD
TO THE SAVED ADDRESS   [3] SPECI
FY YOUR OWN ADDRESS."
   260 INPUT "CHOICE:";X$: LET V=V
AL X$: IF V<1 OR V>3  THEN  GO T
O 260
```

```
 270 IF V=1 THEN  LET MC=MC-L(A)
: LET MCL=MCL+L(A): LET S=MC: GO
TO 300
 280 IF V=2 THEN  LET S=S(A): GO
TO 300
 290 INPUT "LOAD TO ADDRESS.";S
 300 GO SUB 450: LOAD A$(A)CODE
S,L(A): LET NB=NB+1: LET B$(NB)=
A$(A): LET T(NB)=S: LET M(NB)=L(
A): GO SUB 470: GO SUB 430: GO T
O 100
 310 REM SET UP HEADER READER
 320 RESTORE : FOR A=0  TO 11: R
EAD B: POKE 23296+A,B: NEXT A
 330 DATA 221,33,224,91,17,17,0,
175,55,195,86,5
 340 RETURN
 350 REM READ HEADER
 360 RANDOMIZE USR 23296
 370 LET N$="": FOR A=0 TO 9: LE
T N$=N$+CHR$ PEEK (23521+A): NEX
T A: REM FILENAME
 380 LET L=PEEK 23531+256*PEEK 2
3532: REM LENGTH
 390 LET S=PEEK 23533+256*PEEK 2
3534: REM START ADDRESS
 410 POKE 23692,-1: PRINT A$(A);
TAB 14;S(A);TAB 27;L(A): RETURN
 420 LET RT=PEEK 23730+256*PEEK
23731: RETURN
 430 PRINT ''"START OF M.C. AREA=
";RT+1'"ROUTINES START AT ADDRES
S";MC'"TOTAL LENGTH OF ROUTINES=
";MCL''
 440 RETURN
 450 INPUT "": PRINT #0;"START T
HE TAPE!!!": RETURN
 460 REM LIST LOADED ROUTINES
 470 PRINT TAB 8; INVERSE 1;"ROU
TINES LOADED:"'': PRINT " FILENA
ME";TAB 13;"AT ADDRESS";TAB 26;"
LENGTH"''
 480 FOR Y=1 TO NB
 490 PRINT B$(Y);TAB 14;T(Y);TAB
27;M(Y)
 500 NEXT Y: PRINT : RETURN
 510 REM CALL THIS WITH GOTO 520
TO LIST AND SAVE ALL THE ROUTIN
ES CURRENTLY LOADED IN THE M.C.
AREA
 520 GO SUB 470: GO SUB 430
 530 INPUT "FILE NAME?";X$
 540 SAVE X$CODE MC,MCL
```

```
550 PRINT "TO LOAD THE ROUTINES
, USE"''; BRIGHT 1;"CLEAR ";MC-1
;": LOAD """;X$;"""CODE ";MC;","
;MCL
560 INPUT "DO YOU WISH TO VERIF
Y (Y/N)?";A$: IF A$<>"Y" THEN   S
TOP
570 VERIFY X$CODE
```

When 'Routine Selector' is first RUN it automatically reserves
a machine code area of 3000 bytes at the top of memory, and
sets up several arrays which store the names, addresses and
lengths of the routines found and those loaded. For this reason
you should only RUN the program once, or you will end up
clearing all the arrays and trying to reserve another 3000
bytes, which is not possible on a 16K machine. To re-enter the
program after a BREAK, use GOTO 100.

In its standard form, the program will read and load up to 50
routines into 3000 bytes of memory. In the unlikely event that
you need more, variable F in line 70 controls the maximum
number of routines, and increasing 3000 and 3001 in line 60 by
the same amount will lengthen the M.C. area. If at any time you
want to clear the machine code area, then use the command CLEAR
32599 (16K) or CLEAR 65367 (48K). You will then be able to RUN
the program again if you wish.

When you have selected all of your routines, press "s" to get
out of the catalogue or "Break" if the program is trying to
read another header. Then type "GOTO 520" and put a blank tape
in the recorder, ready to SAVE the block of routines. You will
be asked for a file name, the program will save the block and
then present you with the EXACT Basic line necessary to make
room for and load back the toolkit from tape during your own
program. It is well worth noting this down!

You are regularly presented with a list of the routines loaded
into memory and their new addresses during the program. To get
this list from 'immediate' mode, type

                    GOSUB 470

To get a list of all the routines found on tape (the catalog),
type

                    GOTO 100

You will need the list of start addresses from the first GOSUB
in order to call the routines with USR, so note them down! You
are now fully equipped to use the rest of this book: So on with
the routines!

ROUTINES FOR THE ATTRIBUTES

CHAPTER 3
COLOURFUL OPERATIONS ON THE ATTRIBUTES

As you probably know, you can choose one of eight colours on
the Spectrum for the INK and PAPER. You can also specify
whether the printing is BRIGHT or FLASHing. The one major
problem, however, is that in BASIC you cannot easily change any
of these ATTRIBUTES relating to a previously PRINTed character,
without rePRINTing it using the new INK, PAPER, BRIGHT and
FLASH values.

The following routine is a multi-purpose routine which allows
you to change the attributes instantly, operating on a
specified rectangle of the screen without affecting any text or
graphics therein. I have called the routine "SCREENOP".

USING SCREENOP.

The routine operates on a specified rectangle of the screen,
using the usual PRINT AT coordinates.

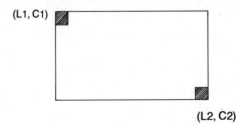

17

Referring to the diagram, we enter the coordinates (L1, C1) of
the character position that forms the top left hand corner, and
the coordinates (L2, C2) of the character position that forms
the bottom right hand corner of the rectangle in which we want
to change the attributes.

POKE 23332, L1 : POKE 23333, C1
POKE 23334, L2 : POKE 23335, C2

All of the colours on the Spectrum are derived from the three
primary colours: green, blue and red. Their codes are:

1 = Blue
2 = Red
4 = Green

The other colours are made up as follows:

Colour		Code
Black	= nothing	0
Magenta	= Blue + Red	1 + 2 = 3
Cyan	= Blue + Green	1 + 4 = 5
Yellow	= Red + Green	2 + 4 = 6
White	= Red + Green + Blue	1 + 2 + 4 = 7

SCREENOP can perform any one of four operations on any of the
various attributes. I will give these attributes a value:

Blue ink   1
Red ink   2
Green ink   4
Blue paper   8
Red paper   16
Green paper   32
BRIGHT   64
FLASH   128

The four possible operations are: turn the attribute "on".
turn the attribute "off".
alter the attribute.
leave the attribute as it is.

You need to poke the data into three seperate addresses, as
follows:

POKE 23328, (sum of values of attributes to
remain unaltered)
POKE 23329, (sum of values of attributes to be
turned "on")
POKE 23331, (sum of values of attributes to be
altered)

By "altering" the part, I mean turning it "on" if it's "off",
and vice versa. There is one important point to remember: if
you wish to alter, or COMPLEMENT one part of the attribute then
you must also include it in the first POKE (otherwise the
attribute will be turned "on" or "off" according to the second
POKE).

EXAMPLE

You wish to highlight a rectangle (brightness "on"), leave any
cyan ink that may occur (leave blue and green ink as they are),
turn all the red ink "on" and complement (alter) all of the
paper and the FLASH attributes. For this you must

          POKE 23328, (1 + 4) + (8 + 16 + 32 + 128)
          POKE 23329, 64 + 2
          POKE 23331, 8 + 16 + 32 + 128

To   run the machine code, use
                  RAND USR (first address of routine)
or   LET L = USR

Here is the routine itself. Enter it using 'hexload' and then
if you wish, enter the spectacular demonstration program.

```
HEX.        ;SCREENOP LENGTH: 95 BYTES
21205B   START  LD    HL,5B20H    ;COMPLEMENT MASK THEN
7E              LD    A,(HL)      ;AND THE NEW ATTRIBUTES.
2F              CPL
23              INC   HL
A6              AND   (HL)
23              INC   HL
77              LD    (HL),A      ;STORE THE RESULT (1)
23              INC   HL
23              INC   HL
46              LD    B,(HL)      ;FIND L1
23              INC   HL
23              INC   HL
7E              LD    A,(HL)      ;FIND L2
FE18            CP    24          ;CHECK THAT L2 IS IN RANGE
D0              RET   NC          ;RETURN IF NOT.
90              SUB   B           ;(L2-L1)=
D8              RET   C           ;RETURN IF NEGATIVE
3C              INC   A           ;(L2-L1)+1=LENGTH OF
F5              PUSH  AF          ;RECTANGLE (LINES)
04              INC   B           ;IS L1 ZERO?
05              DEC   B
E5              PUSH  HL
21005B          LD    HL,5800H
2806            JR    Z,HOP       ;IF SO THEN YOU DONT NEED
112000   NXT1   LD    DE,0020H    ;TO DESCEND TO TOP LINE OF
19              ADD   HL,DE       ;RECTANGLE
10FA            DJNZ  NXT1
EB       HOP    EX    DE,HL
E1              POP   HL
D5              PUSH  DE
```

19

```
23            INC     HL
7E            LD      A,(HL)      ;FIND C2
FE20          CP      32          ;IS C2 IN RANGE?
3803          JR      C,OK        ;IF NOT THEN RETURN
C1            POP     BC
C1    ERRSTOP POP     BC
C9            RET
2B    OK      DEC     HL
2B            DEC     HL
4E            LD      C,(HL)      ;FIND C1.
E1            POP     HL          ;ADVANCE TO TOP LEFT CORNER
09            ADD     HL,BC       ;OF RECTANGLE.
91            SUB     C           ;(C2-C1)=
38F6          JR      C,ERRSTOP   ;RETURN IF NEGATIVE.
3C            INC     A           ;(C2-C1)+1=WIDTH OF
47            LD      B,A         ;RECTANGLE (COLUMNS).
3E20          LD      A,32        ;FIND THE GAP FROM THE
90            SUB     B           ;RIGHT SIDE OF ONE
5F            LD      E,A         ;RECTANGLE LINE TO THE
1600          LD      D,0         ;LEFT SIDE OF THE NEXT
C5    NXTLINE PUSH    BC          ;LINE.
D5            PUSH    DE
3A235B        LD      A,(5B23H)   ;THE COMPLEMENT BYTE (1)
57            LD      D,A
3A205B  NXT2  LD      A,(5B20H)   ;MASK
5F            LD      E,A
7E            LD      A,(HL)      ;TAKE ATTRIBUTES.
AA            XOR     D           ;COMPLEMENT WITH BYTE (1)
A3            AND     E           ;AND (THE MASK BYTE) TO
5F            LD      E,A         ;GIVE RESULT (2).
3A225B        LD      A,(5B21H)
83            ADD     A,E         ;ADD RESULT (1) TO (2)
77            LD      (HL),A      ;REPLACE ATTRIBUTES.
23            INC     HL          ;REPEAT FOR REST OF THIS
10F0          DJNZ    NXT2        ;LINE OF THE RECTANGLE.
D1            POP     DE
19            ADD     HL,DE       ;JUMP TO THE NEXT LINE OF
C1            POP     BC          ;THE RECTANGLE.
F1            POP     AF
3D            DEC     A           ;REPEAT UNTIL THE LAST LINE
C8            RET     Z           ;OF THE RECTANGLES IS DONE.
F5            PUSH    AF
18E1          JR      NXTLINE
              END
```

Here is the demonstration program:

```
10 REM "Screenop" Demonstrati
on
20 REM DEFINE USR GRAPHIC
30 FOR A=0 TO 7
40 POKE USR "A"+A,85+85*(A/2=I
NT (A/2))
50 NEXT A
60 REM FILL SCREEN
70 FOR A=1 TO 704: PRINT CHR$
144;: NEXT A
```

```
   80 PRINT #0;AT 0,0;: FOR a=1
TO 64
   85 PRINT #0;CHR$ 144;: NEXT a
   90 LET SCREENOP=65200
  100 PRINT AT 8,10;"SUPERCHARGE"
;AT 10,13;"YOUR";
  105 PRINT AT 12,11;"SPECTRUM"
  110 RANDOMIZE
  120 REM DEFINE RECTANGLE
  130 REM (L1,C1)
  140 LET A=INT (RND*24): LET B=I
NT (RND*32)
  150 POKE 23332,A: POKE 23333,B
  160 REM (L2,C2)
  170 POKE 23334,A+INT (RND*(24-A
))
  175 POKE 23335,B+INT (RND*(32-B
))
  180 REM RANDOM OPERATION
  190 POKE 23328,INT (RND*256)
  200 POKE 23329,INT (RND*256)
  210 POKE 23331,INT (RND*256)
  220 LET L=USR SCREENOP
  230 GO TO 140
```

The program makes fairly random operations on a fairly random
rectangle of the screen. Lines 15 to 50 define a 'chess-board'
character (graphics U) and fill the screen with it: this allows
you to produce up to 36 colours (or shades of grey) by
combining paper and ink colours and is particularly effective
on a colour TV. Line 70 defines the beginning of the routine:
you must change this number according to where you store the
routine.

APPLICATIONS

The routine can operate on any area from one character up to
all twenty-four lines of the screen. One possibility would be
to print a message using a different set of attributes to its
surroundings and then 'alter' every attribute of the entire
screen continually, using a PAUSE of around 30 between
alterations to make the screen bearable (do not try this if you
suffer from epileptic fits)!

SCREENOP 2

This routine is a minaturised version of SCREENOP: it operates
in the same way but only on the whole screen (including the
bottom two 'EDIT' lines).

USING SCREENOP 2

Use the same 'colour' POKEs and values as for SCREENOP, but do
not define a rectangle. The routine is nearly a quarter the
length of SCREENOP and only requires three POKEs to operate it,
so it should be used whenever the more elaborate 'rectangle'
facility is not required.

```
HEX.           ;SCREENOP2 LENGTH: 27 BYTES
ED4B205B  START   LD   BC,(5B20H)    ;AND THE COMPLEMENT OF THE
79                LD   A,C           ;MASK WITH THE NEW
2F                CPL                ;ATTRIBUTES.
A0                AND  B
47                LD   B,A
210058            LD   HL,5800H      ;HL=START OF ATTRIBUTES.
ED5B225B          LD   DE,(5B21H)    ;D IS THE COMPLEMENTER.
7E        NXTATT  LD   A,(HL)        ;TAKE ATTRIBUTES
AA                XOR  D             ;OPERATE
A1                AND  C
80                ADD  A,B
77                LD   (HL),A        ;REPLACE ATTRIBUTES.
23                INC  HL            ;INCREMENT COUNTER.
7C                LD   A,H           ;END OF ATTRIBUTES?
FE5B              CP   5BH
38F5              JR   C,NXTATT      ;IF NOT, NEXT ATTRIBUTE
C9                RET                ;RETURN TO BASIC.
                  END
```

CHAPTER 4
INVERTING THE ATTRIBUTES

This routine takes all the 'INK' and 'PAPER' of each character
in the specified screen rectangle and swaps them around (e.g.
red INK on green PAPER becomes green INK on red PAPER). The
rectangle is specified in exactly the same way as for SCREENOP,
as is the case for all of the routines that work on a
colour-byte or 'attributes' rectangle. Apart from the four
POKEs described in the previous routine (23332 to 23335...), no
other preparation is required before calling the routine with
"LET C = USR (start address)". I have also included a
super-fast, super-short, whole screen version which requires no
POKEs whatsoever.

```
HEX.          ;INVERSE RECTANGLE  LENGTH: 78 BYTES
ED4B245B  START  LD    BC,(5B24H)              .
2A265B           LD    HL,(5B26H)
7D               LD    A,L           ;CHECK FOR LEGALITY OF
FE18             CP    18H           ;L2 AND L1.
D0               RET   NC
91               SUB   C
D8               RET   C
5F               LD    E,A
7C               LD    A,H           ;CHECK FOR LEGALITY OF
FE20             CP    20H           ;C2 AND C1.
D0               RET   NC
90               SUB   B
D8               RET   C
57               LD    D,A
14               INC   D             ;D=WIDTH OF RECTANGLE.
```

```
1C              INC   E          ;E=LENGTH OF RECTANGLE.
D5              PUSH  DE         ;STORE THEM.
210058          LD    HL,5800H   ;FIND FIRST LINE OF
AF              XOR   A          ;RECTANGLE.
B9              CP    C
112000          LD    DE,20H
2804            JR    Z,HOP1
19        NXT1  ADD   HL,DE
0D              DEC   C
20FC            JR    NZ,NXT1
B8        HOP1  CP    B          ;FIND TOP LEFTHAND CORNER
2803            JR    Z,HOP2     ;OF RECTANGLE.
23        NXT2  INC   HL
10FD            DJNZ  NXT2
C1        HOP2  POP   BC         ;B=WIDTH, C=LENGTH
D5        NXTLINE PUSH DE
E5              PUSH  HL
C5              PUSH  BC
3E07      NXT3  LD    A,7        ;TAKE INK.
A6              AND   (HL)
0F              RRCA
0F              RRCA
4F              LD    C,A        ;STORE IT.
3E38            LD    A,38H      ;TAKE PAPER.
A6              AND   (HL)
81              ADD   A,C        ;INK AND PAPER ARE NOW IN
0F              RRCA             ;REVERSE ORDER.
0F              RRCA
0F              RRCA
4F              LD    C,A
3EC0            LD    A,0C0H     ;TAKE FLASH AND BRIGHT
A6              AND   (HL)       ;BITS.
81              ADD   A,C        ;PUT THEM IN THE NEW
77              LD    (HL),A     ;ATTRIBUTE UNCHANGED AND
23              INC   HL         ;STORE NEW ATTRIBUTE.
10EA            DJNZ  NXT3       ;NEXT CHARACTER.
C1              POP   BC
E1              POP   HL
D1              POP   DE
0D              DEC   C
19              ADD   HL,DE
20E0            JR    NZ,NXTLINE ;REPEAT UNTIL END OF
C9              RET              ;RECTANGLE. RETURN TO
                END              ;BASIC.
```

There now follows a mind-boggling demonstration program for
INVERSE. Remember to alter the number in line 30 according to
where you have located the routine. To see the program at
neck-breaking full speed remove the PAUSE statement in line
190.

```
10 REM INVERSE RECTANGLE
20 REM DEMONSTRATION
30 LET REVERSE=65200
40 LET A=INT (RND*8): LET B=IN
T (RND*8): IF A=B THEN  GO TO 40
```

```
  50 PAPER A: INK B: BRIGHT RND:
CLS
  60 PRINT AT 10,10;"Look into m
y";AT 11,10;">>>>eyes<<<<"
  70 LET B=0: LET C=10
  80 GO SUB 120: REM ZOOM OUT
  90 LET B=C: LET C=0
 100 GO SUB 120: REM ZOOM IN
 110 GO TO 40
 120 FOR D=B  TO C STEP SGN (C-B
)
 130 REM DEFINE RECTANGLE
 140 POKE 23332,10-D: REM L1
 150 POKE 23333,10-D: REM C1
 160 POKE 23334,11+D: REM L2
 170 POKE 23335,21+D: REM C2
 180  LET L=USR REVERSE
 190 PAUSE 4: NEXT D
 200 RETURN
```

FULL-SCREEN INVERSE

Here is the whole-screen version of INVERSE that I mentioned
earlier. No POKEs needed, and it occupies a mere 29 bytes (this
compares with line 40 of the above 'Inverse Demonstration'
program, which takes 51 bytes of memory). You will probably
need to use it with a PAUSE if in a 'flash' loop.

```
HEX.          ;FULL-SCREEN INVERSE  LENGTH: 29 BYTES
210058   START  LD·  HL,5800H      ;BEGINNING OF ATTRIBUTES.
3E07     NXTATT LD   A,7
A6              AND  (HL)           ;TAKE INK.
0F              RRCA
0F              RRCA
57              LD   D,A            ;STORE IT.
3E38            LD   A,38H
A6              AND  (HL)           ;TAKE PAPER.
82              ADD  A,D            ;PUT IN FRONT OF INK.
0F              RRCA                ;INK AND PAPER ARE NOW
0F              RRCA                ;REVERSED.
57              LD   D,A            ;STORE THEM. TAKE
3EC0            LD   A,0C0H         ;FLASH AND BRIGHT BITS.
A6              AND  (HL)
82              ADD  A,D            ;COMBINE WITH LAST RESULT.
77              LD   (HL),A         ;STORE NEW ATTRIBUTES.
23              INC  HL             ;INCREMENT COUNTER. ARE
7C              LD   A,H            ;WE AT THE PRINTER BUFFER?
FE5B            CP   5BH
38E8            JR   C,NXTATT       ;IF NOT, THEN NEXT
C9              RET                 ;ATTRIBUTE. RETURN TO BASIC.
                END
```

CHAPTER 5
SCROLLING THE ATTRIBUTES IN ALL DIRECTIONS.

The following set of routines allows you to 'scroll' the colour
bytes of the screen in any of the four directions LEFT, RIGHT,
UP and DOWN. There are two routines for each direction: the
first one allows you to scroll any rectangle of the screen
area, and the second, shorter and simpler type will work on the
entire screen only.

USING THE ROUTINES

For the 'rectangle' routines, define the rectangle in the same
way as for SCREENOP (Chapter 3), using the same POKEs.

For all of the routines, you have three options:

0. 'leave' the line or column which is left behind by the
scroll (e.g. the bottom line when scrolling the screen upwards)
as it is;

1. 'roll' the line or column which would be deleted by the
scroll back into the position left behind by the scroll (in
this way you could continuously rotate a rectangle of
attributes by 'scROLL—ing' them repeatedly in one direction);

2. 'fill' the line or column left behind by the scroll with a
new attribute.

First define the rectangle if necessary, then execute the
appropriate POKE(s):

```
                        ⎧ 0 to 'leave'
     POKE 23340,        ⎨ 1 to 'roll'
                        ⎩ 2 to 'fill'
```

POKE 23341, sum of values of attributes to be used when
'filling'.

VALUES OF ATTRIBUTES WHEN 'ON':

Flash	= 128	Blue paper	= 8
Bright	= 64	Green ink	= 4
Green paper	= 32	Red ink	= 2
Red paper	= 16	Blue ink	= 1

APPLICATIONS

If you've ever watched ITV's "Crossroads", or even seen the
credits come up as you defected from the other side to see if
it had finished, then you will have seen the unusual manner in
which the credits traverse the screen. An interesting exercise
would be to imitate this motion with a 'BRIGHT' rectangle that
approaches the centre of the screen from one side, stays in the
middle to highlight a message of some kind, and then scrolls
off by way of another side of the screen. There are many
occasions when routines like these can enhance a program, so
I'll leave further applications to your imagination.

Here are the routines:

Routines 1 and 2 : Scroll Attribute Rectangle Right and Left

The listing below is to scroll a rectangle to the RIGHT. To
change the direction to LEFT, alter the lines labelled (i),
(ii), and (iii) as follows:

	Mnemonic	Hex
(i)	NOP	00
(ii)	INC HL	23
(iii)	LDIR	EDB0

To change the routine from one direction to the other during a
program (if you prefer not to store the two seperate routines)
then do the following:

               LET S = [start of routine]

LEFT	RIGHT
POKE S+23, 0	POKE S+23, 68
POKE S+55, 35	POKE S+55, 43
POKE S+57, 176	POKE S+57, 184

The above method, incidentally, takes about 70 bytes of RAM, so
there is very little to choose between that and storing the hex.
routines seperately (if you need to use the above POKEs more
than once then it is "cheaper" to store the routines seperately
instead).

Run the routines with the usual command:

LET C = USR S

```
HEX.              ;RIGHTSCROLL ATTRIBUTE RECTANGLE  LENGTH: 81 BYTES
                  ORG      6000H
ED4B245B  START   LD   BC,(5B24H)     ;C=L1, B=C1
2A265B            LD   HL,(5B26H)     ;L=L2, H=C2
7D                LD   A,L            ;CHECK FOR LEGALITY OF
FE18              CP   18H            ;L1 AND L2, RETURN IF
D0                RET  NC             ;ILLEGAL COORDINATES.
91                SUB  C
D8                RET  C
57                LD   D,A
7C                LD   A,H            ;CHECK FOR LEGALITY OF C1
FE20              CP   20H            ;AND C2, RETURN IF ILLEGAL
D0                RET  NC             ;COORDINATES.
90                SUB  B
D8                RET  C
5F                LD   E,A            ;E=WIDTH OF RECTANGLE-1
14                INC  D              ;D=LENGTH OF RECTANGLE.
D5                PUSH DE
44          (i)   LD   B,H            ;(I) SEE NOTES ABOVE
210058            LD   HL,5800H       ;FIND THE TOP LINE OF THE
AF                XOR  A              ;'SCROLL' RECTANGLE.
112000            LD   DE,20H
B9                CP   C
2804              JR   Z,HOP1
19        NXT1    ADD  HL,DE
0D                DEC  C
20FC              JR   NZ,NXT1
B8        HOP1    CP   B              ;FIND TOPLEFT (LEFTSCROLL)
2803              JR   Z,HOP2         ;OR TOPRIGHT (RIGHTSCROLL)
23        NXT2    INC  HL             ;CORNER OF RECTANGLE.
10FD              DJNZ NXT2
C1        HOP2    POP  BC             ;BC=WIDTH OF RECTANGLE-1
C5        NXTLINE PUSH BC
47                LD   B,A            ;SET UP THE VARIABLES DE
D5                PUSH DE             ;AND HL, READY TO SCROLL
54                LD   D,H            ;THE TOP LINE OF THE
5D                LD   E,L            ;RECTANGLE.
D5                PUSH DE
B9                CP   C
1A                LD   A,(DE)
2803              JR   Z,HOP3
2B         (ii)   DEC  HL            ;(II) SEE NOTES ABOVE
EDB8      (iii)   LDDR               ;(III) SEE NOTES ABOVE
ED4B2C5B  HOP3    LD   BC,(5B2CH)     ;HAVING SCROLLED THE
67                LD   H,A            ;LINE, DECIDE WHETHER TO...
79                LD   A,C
FE01              CP   1
3805              JR   C,LEAVIT
7C                LD   A,H
2801              JR   Z,ROLL
78        FILL    LD   A,B            ;... 'FILL' IT, ...
```

28

```
12            ROLL    LD    (DE),A    ;... 'ROLL' IT, ...
E1            LEAVIT  POP   HL        ;... OR 'LEAVE' IT.
D1                    POP   DE        ;PREPARE FOR NEXT LINE OF
C1                    POP   BC        ;RECTANGLE.
19                    ADD   HL,DE
AF                    XOR   A
10DD                  DJNZ  NXTLINE   ;REPEAT UNTIL BOTTOM OF
C9                    RET             ;RECTANGLE IS DONE, THEN
                      END             ;RETURN TO BASIC.
```

Here is a little 'demo' program.

```
  10 REM RIGHT SCROLL ATTRIBUTES
  15 REM DEMONSTRATION
  20 LET RIGHTSCROLL=65200: REM
INSERT YOUR OWN START OF ROUTINE
  30  BORDER 2: CLS : FOR A=0 TO
21
 '40 FOR B=0 TO 7
  50 PRINT  PAPER B; INK 7-B;"
   "
  60 NEXT B
  70 NEXT A
  80 PRINT  INK 8; PAPER 8;AT 10
,6;"I am not a test card"
  90 REM  DEFINE RECTANGLE
 100 POKE 23332,4: POKE 23334,17
: REM L1,L2
 110 POKE 23340,1: REM "ROLL"
 120 LET A=INT (RND*7)*4: REM C1
 130 LET B=A+7+INT (RND*(6-INT (
A/4)))*4: REM C2
 140 POKE 23333,A: POKE 23335,B
 150 FOR A=1 TO 4
 160 LET L=USR RIGHTSCROLL
 170 PAUSE 2: NEXT A
 180 PAUSE 30
 190 GO TO 120
```

In line 50 " " = space. You should plug in the appropriate
value in line 20 to tell the Spectrum where the routine starts.
On running the program the screen is filled with eight coloured
stripes, the centre portions of which are then visually
'shuffled' by scrolling a random number of these portions four
places to the right. You may like to try getting the program to
randomly scroll left and right by randomly changing the three
POKEs needed to alter the routine from one direction to the
other (remember you must use only one set of these POKEs at a
time: DO NOT mix them).

Routines 3 and 4: SCROLL ALL ATTRIBUTES RIGHT OR LEFT

If you only need to scroll the whole screen (including the EDIT
lines), then the following two routines can be used. Since you
do not define a rectangle, the only POKEs required for these
routines are 23340 and 23341.

```
HEX.          ;RIGHTSCROLL ATTRIBUTES  LENGTH: 34 BYTES
11FF5A   START  LD     DE,5AFFH     ;BOTTOM-RIGHT CORNER
011F00   NXTLINE LD    BC,001FH
62              LD     H,D
6B              LD     L,E
2B              DEC    HL
1A              LD     A,(DE)
EDB8            LDDR                 ;SCROLL THE BOTTOM LINE.
ED4B2C5B        LD     BC,(5B2CH)   ;* C=(23340), B=(23341)
67              LD     H,A
79              LD     A,C
FE01            CP     1
3805            JR     C,LEAVIT     ;IF C=0 THEN 'LEAVE'
7C              LD     A,H
2801            JR     Z,ROLL       ;IF C=1 THEN 'ROLL'
78       FILL   LD     A,B          ;ELSE 'FILL'
12       ROLL   LD     (DE),A
1B       LEAVIT DEC    DE           ;FIND NEXT LINE UP.
7A              LD     A,D          ;HAVE WE FINISHED?
FE57            CP     57H
20E2            JR     NZ,NXTLINE   ;IF NOT, THEN NXTLINE.
C9              RET                  ;RETURN TO BASIC.
                END
```

```
HEX.          ;LEFTSCROLL ATTRIBUTES  LENGTH: 34 BYTES
110058   START  LD     DE,5800H     ;TOP LEFTHAND CORNER.
011F00   NXTLINE LD    BC,001FH
62              LD     H,D
6B              LD     L,E
23              INC    HL
1A              LD     A,(DE)
EDB0            LDIR                 ;SCROLL TOP LINE.
ED4B2C5B        LD     BC,(5B2CH)   ;* C=(23340), B=(23341)
67              LD     H,A
79              LD     A,C
FE01            CP     1
3805            JR     C,LEAVIT     ;IF C=0 THEN 'LEAVE'
7C              LD     A,H
2801            JR     Z,ROLL       ;IF C=1 THEN 'ROLL'
78       FILL   LD     A,B          ;ELSE 'FILL'
12       ROLL   LD     (DE),A
13       LEAVIT INC    DE           ;FIND NEXT LINE DOWN.
7A              LD     A,D          ;HAS IT REACHED THE PRINTER
FE5B            CP     5BH          ;BUFFER?
20E2            JR     NZ,NXTLINE   ;IF NOT, THEN NXTLINE.
C9              RET                  ;RETURN TO BASIC.
                END
```

ROUTINES 5 AND 6: SCROLL ATTRIBUTE WINDOW DOWN OR UP

The listing below is to scroll a rectangle of the attributes
DOWN. To change this to UP, alter the lines (i) and (ii) as
follows:

```
                                         HEX.
            (i) NOP                       00
            (ii) LD HL, 2020H             21 20 00
```

30

If you do not wish to store them as two seperate routines, you can convert one to the other as follows:

LET S = (start of routine)

DOWN	UP
POKE S + 22, 77	POKE S + 22, 0
POKE S + 61, 224	POKE S + 61, 32
POKE S + 62, 255	POKE S + 62, 0

As usual, run with

LET C = USR S

```
HEX.        ;DOWNSCROLL ATTRIBUTE RECTANGLE  LENGTH: 105 BYTES
ED4B245B  START  LD    BC,(5B24H)   ;C=L1, B=C1
2A265B           LD    HL,(5B26H)   ;L=L2, H=C2
7D               LD    A,L          ;CHECK FOR LEGALITY OF L1
FE18             CP    18H          ;AND L2, RETURN IF ILLEGAL
D0               RET   NC           ;COORDINATES.
91               SUB   C
D8               RET   C
57               LD    D,A
7C               LD    A,H          ;CHECK FOR LEGALITY OF
FE20             CP    20H          ;C1 AND C2, RETURN IF
D0               RET   NC           ;ILLEGAL COORDINATES.
90               SUB   B
D8               RET   C
5F               LD    E,A
1C               INC   E            ;E=WIDTH OF RECTANGLE.
4D          (i)  LD    C,L          ;(I) SEE NOTES ABOVE
D5               PUSH  DE           ;FIND THE TOP (UPSCROLL)
210058           LD    HL,5800H     ;OR BOTTOM (DOWNSCROLL)
AF               XOR   A            ;LINE OF RECTANGLE.
B9               CP    C
2807             JR    Z,HOP1
112000           LD    DE,20H
19        NXT1   ADD   HL,DE
0D               DEC   C
20FC             JR    NZ,NXT1
B8        HOP1   CP    B            ;ADVANCE TO TOP-LEFT OR
2803             JR    Z,HOP2       ;BOTTOM-LEFT CORNER.
23        NXT2   INC   HL
10FD             DJNZ  NXT2
C1        HOP2   POP   BC
C5               PUSH  BC
47               LD    B,A          ;BC=WIDTH OF RECTANGLE.
E5               PUSH  HL           ;STORE THE LINE OF THE
11E05B           LD    DE,5BE0H     ;RECTANGLE ABOUT TO BE
EDB0             LDIR               ;ERASED.
D1               POP   DE
C1               POP   BC
B8               CP    B
280D             JR    Z,DONE
C5        NXTLINE PUSH BC           ;BEGIN ACTUAL SCROLLING, BY
47               LD    B,A          ;SETTING UP HL AND DE,...
```

31

```
21E0FF    (ii) LD    HL,0FFE0H    ;(II)
19             ADD   HL,DE
E5             PUSH  HL
EDB0           LDIR               ;THEN SCROLLING....
D1             POP   DE
C1             POP   BC
10F3           DJNZ  NXTLINE      ;ONE LINE AT A TIME UNTIL
C5        DONE PUSH  BC           ;THE WHOLE RECTANGLE IS
2A2C5B         LD    HL,(5B2CH)   ;DONE. DECIDE WHETHER TO
7D             LD    A,L          ;'LEAVE', 'FILL' OR 'ROLL'.
FE01           CP    1
380F           JR    C,CLEANUP
2007           JR    NZ,FILL
21E05B    ROLL LD    HL,5BE0H     ;'ROLL' BY RETURNING THE
EDB0           LDIR               ;STORED LINE AND PUTTING
1806           JR    CLEANUP      ;IT IN THE APPROPRIATE
EB        FILL EX    DE,HL        ;PLACE. THEN GO TO THE
                                  ;'CLEANUP' AREA.
72        NXT3 LD    (HL),D       ;'FILL' THE LINE EXPOSED
23             INC   HL           ;BY THE SCROLL.
0D             DEC   C
20FB           JR    NZ,NXT3
C1     CLEANUP POP   BC           ;'CLEANUP' THE PRINTER
21E05B         LD    HL,5BE0H     ;BUFFER. USED TO STORE A
70        NXT4 LD    (HL),B       ;LINE OF THE RECTANGLE.
0D             DEC   C
23             INC   HL
20FB           JR    NZ,NXT4
C9             RET                ;RETURN TO BASIC.
               END
```

Warning: all of the 'downscroll' and 'upscroll' routines make use of the printer buffer (the area where LPRINT, LLIST and COPY information is temporarily stored on its way to the printer), so anything stored in the printer buffer will be lost on using the routines. This does not stop you from using the printer; just be sure that anything LPRINTed before you 'call' the routines has actually been sent out to the printer.

Here is a demonstration program for the 'downscroll' routine. If the colours make you ill then feel free to change them: the program was developed with a black and white TV. Line 30 should be altered appropriately to the beginning of the 'downscroll' routine (e.g. if your routine is at address 32400, then line 30 should read "LET DOWNSCROLL = 32400"). You will find that the program generates a recursive, 'kaleidoscopic' pattern.

```
10 REM DOWNSCROLL ATTRIBUTES
20 REM DEMONSTRATION
30 LET DOWNSCROLL=65200
40 REM PREPARE SCREEN
50 BORDER 7: CLS : INVERSE 1
60 FOR A=0 TO 168 STEP 8
70 PLOT  INK 2; PAPER 2+3*(A>8
0);7,A
```

```
  80 DRAW   INK 2; PAPER 2+3*(A>8
0);241,0
  90 NEXT A: INVERSE O
 100 PRINT   INK 8; PAPER 8;AT 10
,14;"FLIP";AT 11,14;"FLOP"
 110 POKE 23340,1: REM "ROLL"
 120 REM DEFINE RECTANGLE
 130 LET B=0
 140 LET A=1
 150 LET X=INT (B*5/7+0.5)
 160 POKE 23332,10-X: REM L1
 170 POKE 23333,14-B: REM C1
 180 POKE 23334,11+X: REM L2
 190 POKE 23335,17+B: REM C2
 200 FOR N=0 TO X
 210 RANDOMIZE USR DOWNSCROLL
 220 PAUSE 6: NEXT N
 230 LET B=B+A
 240 LET A=A+2*((B=0)-(B=14))
 250 PAUSE 50: GO TO 150
```

ROUTINES 7 AND 8: SCROLL ALL ATTRIBUTES DOWN OR UP

These routines are for use when the more lengthy 'rectangle'
routines are unnecessary. They work on all 24 lines of the
screen and as with the 'rectangle' routines, the contents of
the printer buffer are erased along with anything not yet
passed out to the printer. Use the usual POKEs, 23340 and
23341.

```
HEX.        ;DOWNSCROLL ATTRIBUTES  LENGTH: 54 BYTES
012000          LD    BC,20H      ;MOVE THE BOTTOM LINE
21FF5A          LD    HL,5AFFH    ;INTO THE PRINTER BUFFER.
11FF5B          LD    DE,5BFFH
D5              PUSH  DE
E5              PUSH  HL
EDB8            LDDR
D1              POP   DE          ;NOW MOVE THE REST OF THE
01E002          LD    BC,02E0H    ;ATTRIBUTES DOWN A LINE.
EDB8            LDDR
3A2C5B          LD    A,(5B2CH)   ;A=(23340)
FE01            CP    1           ;DECIDE WHETHER TO ....
012000          LD    BC,20H
3810            JR    C,CLEANUP   ;.. LEAVE TOP LINE,
2006            JR    NZ,FILL     ;FILL IT, OR
E1       ROLL   POP   HL          ;ROLL THE BOTTOM LINE UP
E5              PUSH  HL          ;TO THE TOP.
EDB8            LDDR
1808            JR    CLEANUP
3A2D5B   FILL   LD    A,(5B2DH)   ;A=(23341)
12       NXT    LD    (DE),A      ;FILL TOP LINE WITH A.
1B              DEC   DE
0D              DEC   C
20FB            JR    NZ,NXT
```

```
0620        CLEANUP LD    B,20H      ;CLEANUP THE PRINTER
AF                  XOR   A          ;BUFFER.
E1                  POP   HL
77          NXT2    LD    (HL),A
2B                  DEC   HL
10FC                DJNZ  NXT2
C9                  RET              ;RETURN TO BASIC.
                    END
```

Here's another amazing demonstration program to show off the above routine:

```
 10 REM WHOLE SCREEN DOWN
 20 REM SCROLL OF ATTRIBUTES
 30 REM DEMONSTRATION
 35 LET DOWNSCROLL=65200: POKE
23340,1: REM ROLL
 40 BRIGHT 1: FOR A=0 TO 21
 50 LET B=A-8*INT (A/8)
 60 PRINT  INK 7-B; PAPER B;"AM
AZING TECHNICOLOURED SCROLLING"
 70 NEXT A
 80 FOR A=0 TO 1
 90 PRINT #0;AT A,0; INK 7-A; P
APER A;"AMAZING TECHNICOLOURED S
CROLLING"
100 NEXT A
110 RANDOMIZE USR DOWNSCROLL
120 PAUSE 5: GO TO 110
```

Don't forget to alter the number 65200 in line 35 to the start address of the routine. To produce the top speed, remove the pause statement in line 120 (it then becomes impossible to follow the pattern, since the scrolling will occur more often than a new television frame is displayed). Here is the equivalent upscroll routine:

```
HEX.        ;UPSCROLL ATTRIBUTES  LENGTH: 50 BYTES
210058 START  LD    HL,5800H   ;MOVE THE TOP LINE INTO
11E05B        LD    DE,5BE0H   ;THE PRINTER BUFFER.
D5            PUSH  DE
E5            PUSH  HL
012000        LD    BC,0020H
EDB0          LDIR
D1            POP   DE         ;NOW MOVE THE REST OF THE
01E002        LD    BC,02E0H   ;ATTRIBUTES UP A LINE.
EDB0          LDIR
3A2C5B        LD    A,(5B2CH)  ;A=(23340)
FE01          CP    1          ;DECIDE WHETHER TO ....
012000        LD    BC,20H
380F          JR    C,CLEANUP  ;LEAVE BOTTOM LINE,
2006          JR    NZ,FILL    ;FILL IT, OR
E1     ROLL   POP   HL         ;ROLL THE TOP LINE DOWN
E5            PUSH  HL         ;FROM THE PRINTER BUFFER.
```

34

```
EDB0              LDIR
1807              JR       CLEANUP
3A2D5B    FILL    LD       A,(5B2DH)    ;A=(23341)
12        NXT1    LD       (DE),A       ;FILL BOTTOM LINE WITH A.
1C                INC      E
20FC              JR       NZ,NXT1
E1        CLEANUP POP      HL           ;CLEANUP THE PRINTER
70        NXT2    LD       (HL),B       ;BUFFER.
2C                INC      L
20FC              JR       NZ,NXT2
C9                RET                   ;RETURN TO BASIC.
                  END
```

The same demonstration program used for 'Downscroll' will work
with 'Upscroll'.

ROUTINES FOR THE TEXT AND GRAPHICS

CHAPTER 6
SCROLLING THE TEXT AND GRAPHICS

I have already provided you with a complete set of routines to
scroll the 'colour' bytes or attributes; here then is a similar
set that will allow you to do the same to the text and graphics
present on the screen.

As for the attribute routines, there are two main types; the
first and most complex routine works on any rectangle of the
screen from one square to the full 24 x 32 size; the second,
shorter routine works only on the whole screen.

USING THE ROUTINES

If you are using a 'rectangle' routine, then you must first
define the rectangle using the same POKEs and in the same
manner as for SCREENOP (see Chapter 3). Text will then only be
scrolled if it is inside the rectangle. As for the attribute
routines, you now have three options:

0. LEAVE the line or column which is 'left behind' by the
scroll (e.g. the bottom line when scrolling upwards) as it is;

1. ROLL the line or column which would be deleted by the
scroll back into the position left behind by the scroll;

2. FILL the line or column left behind by the scroll with one
of 256 patterns.

In the last option, you define the pattern by POKEing into
address 23347 a number between 0 and 255 (both inclusive). This

is most easily accomplished by using the BIN function, as
follows.

Imagine a character square being split into eight horizontal
layers or 'rows'. Each of these rows would then consist of a
line of eight PLOT positions, or 'pixels', thus:

The routine allows you to set each of these pixels to INK (1)
or PAPER (0) and then replaces every row of every character
square of every line or column 'left behind' by the scroll with
the row of pixels that you have defined. In this way a series
of vertical lines is produced whose thickness and spacing
varies according to the row defined. In the diagram, alternate
pixels of the row are INK, and a 'pinstripe trouser' pattern
would be produced during repeated scrolls.

You must POKE 23347 with the 'pattern row' in BIN form:

             POKE 23347, BIN 1 0 1 0 1 0 1 0

To choose which of the three options the routine is to use, use
this command with the appropriate number:

                POKE 23346,   0 to 'LEAVE'
                                 1 to 'ROLL'
                                 2 to 'FILL'

APPLICATIONS

At the end of this chapter you will find a demonstration
program called CRISS-CROSS, which utilises each of the four
'rectangle' text-scrolling routines. The program is a
computer-simulation of a puzzle that has sold in the millions
(and has had a similar number of pictures printed on it). You
have a four-by-four grid with fifteen tiles and one hole in it.
The tiles are numbered from one to fifteen, and are 'jumbled
up' by the computer by randomly and visually interchanging
the 'hole' on the screen with one of its four next-door
neighbours. The computer then leaves you to enter the moves
and restore the tiles to their original positions.

The application above of 'scrolling' the tiles of the puzzle is
only the tip of a spectronic iceberg. You could use the
routines to make a 'plane fly (by scrolling the landscape
underneath it using the 'ROLL' option), or perhaps in the
classic invader-type game to speed up the movement of the block
of invaders, the mother ship, the laser base and possibly even
the bombs and missiles. With the extra speed added by these
routines it should be possible to produce a quite acceptable
game under BASIC control.

COORDINATION WITH ATTRIBUTE ROUTINES

If you wish to combine any of these routines with its
corresponding 'colour' routine, thereby using only one USR call
instead of two seperate ones, then you should follow this
procedure:

1. Write the 'graphic' routine with Hexaid;

2. Immediately afterwards, write the corresponding 'attribute'
routine (so that the attribute routine directly precedes the
graphic routine in memory), changing the last line of the
attribute routine

		HEX.
from	RET	C9
to	NOP	00

The combined routine is now accessed by the USR call

LET L = USR (start of attribute routine).

Now on to the tedious bit we have all come to hate; typing in
the routines.

LEFT AND RIGHT FOR RECTANGLES

RIGHTR (R for rectangle), not surprisingly, scrolls to the
right. To change the routine to 'LEFTR', alter lines (i), (ii)
and (iii) as follows:

	NEW LINE	HEX.
(i)	NOP	00
(ii)	INC HL	23
(iii)	LDIR	ED BO

If you do not want to store the two routines seperately, you
can convert from one to the other during a BASIC program or by
direct commands as follows:

LET R = (start of routine)

LEFT	RIGHT
POKE R + 23, 0	POKE R + 23, 68
POKE R + 44, 35	POKE R + 44, 43
POKE R + 52, 176	POKE R + 52, 184

```
HEX.          ;RIGHTR LENGTH: 89 BYTES
ED4B245B  START  LD    BC,(5B24H)   ;C=L1, B=C1
2A265B           LD    HL,(5B26H)   ;L=L2, H=C2
7D               LD    A,L          ;CHECK FOR ILLEGAL
FE18             CP    18H          ;COORDINATES.
D0               RET   NC
91               SUB   C
D8               RET   C
57               LD    D,A
```

```
7C              LD    A,H
FE20            CP    20H
D0              RET   NC
90              SUB   B
D8              RET   C
5F              LD    E,A        ;E=WIDTH OF RECTANGLE-1
14              INC   D          ;D=NO. OF LINES.
D5              PUSH  DE         ;STORE THEM!
44       (i) LD B,H             ;FIND THE ADDRESS OF
79              LD    A,C        ;(L1,C2), THE TOP - RIGHT
E618            AND   18H        ;CORNER. FIRST FIND WHICH
C640            ADD   A,40H      ;THIRD OF THE SCREEN
67              LD    H,A        ;IT IS IN.
79              LD    A,C
87              ADD   A,A        ;NOW WHICH LINE.....
87              ADD   A,A
87              ADD   A,A
87              ADD   A,A
87              ADD   A,A
80              ADD   A,B
6F              LD    L,A        ;AND FINALLY WHICH COLUMN
C1       NXTROWS POP  BC
C5       NXTLINE PUSH BC
E5              PUSH  HL
54              LD    D,H
5D              LD    E,L
7E              LD    A,(HL)     ;STORE RIGHT-MOST ROW.
2B       (ii) DEC HL
08              EX    AF,AF'
AF              XOR   A
47              LD    B,A        ;BC=WIDTH-1
B9              CP    C          ;IF WIDTH=1 THEN DON'T
2802            JR    Z,HOP1     ;SCROLL.
EDB8     (iii) LDDR             ;SCROLL THE LINE.
2A325B   HOP1   LD   HL,(5B32H) ;DECIDE WHETHER TO...
7D              LD    A,L
FE01            CP    1
3805            JR    C,LEAVIT   ;LEAVE,
7C              LD    A,H
2001            JR    NZ,FILL    ;FILL, OR ELSE...ROLL
08       ROLL   EX   AF,AF'      ;RIGHT-MOST ROW INTO LEFT-
12       FILL   LD   (DE),A      ;MOST. FILL WITH SPECIFIED
E1       LEAVIT POP  HL          ;PATTERN. ONTO THE NEXT
24              INC   H          ;ROW OF EACH CHARACTER.
7C              LD    A,H
E607            AND   7
20DD            JR    NZ,NXTROWS
1120F8          LD    DE,0F820H  ;THEN FIND THE NEXT
19              ADD   HL,DE      ;LINE OF THE RECTANGLE.
7D              LD    A,L
FE20            CP    20H
3003            JR    NC,NOTTHRD
0607            LD    B,7
09              ADD   HL,BC
```

40

```
C1           NOTTHRD POP    BC
10CF                 DJNZ   NXTLINE      ;REPEAT UNTIL LAST LINE HAS
C9                   RET                 ;BEEN SCROLLED, THEN RETURN
                     END                 ;TO BASIC.
```

LEFT AND RIGHT FOR THE WHOLE SCREEN

These two routines work on the whole screen and therefore
require only two POKEs, 23346 and 23347. I have suffixed their
name with "WS" for "whole-screen".

```
HEX.         ;LEFTWS LENGTH: 33 BYTES
210040       START   LD    HL,4000H      ;HL=TOP-LEFT CORNER
011F00       NXTROWS LD    BC,001FH      ;BC=WIDTH OF SCREEN-1
7E                   LD    A,(HL)        ;STORE LEFT-MOST ROW.
54                   LD    D,H
5D                   LD    E,L
23                   INC   HL
EDB0                 LDIR                 ;SCROLL LEFT
08                   EX    AF,AF'
ED4B325B             LD    BC,(5B32H)     ;TEST (23346) AND EITHER...
79                   LD    A,C
FE01                 CP    1
3805                 JR    C,LEAVIT       ;LEAVE OR ELSE
78                   LD    A,B
2001                 JR    NZ,FILL        ;FILL OR
08           ROLL    EX    AF,AF'         ;ROLL
12           FILL    LD    (DE),A
7C           LEAVIT  LD    A,H            ;REPEAT UNTIL WHOLE SCREEN
FE58                 CP    58H            ;IS SCROLLED.
38E3                 JR    C,NXTROWS
C9                   RET                  ;RETURN TO BASIC.
                     END
```

```
HEX.         ;RIGHTWS LENGTH: 33 BYTES
21FF57       START   LD    HL,57FFH      ;HL=BOTTOM-RIGHT CORNER
011F00       NXTROWS LD    BC,001FH      ;BC=WIDTH OF SCREEN-1
7E                   LD    A,(HL)        ;STORE RIGHT-MOST ROW.
54                   LD    D,H
5D                   LD    E,L
2B                   DEC   HL
EDB8                 LDDR                 ;SCROLL RIGHT.
08                   EX    AF,AF'
ED4B325B             LD    BC,(5B32H)     ;TEST (23346) AND EITHER...
79                   LD    A,C
FE01                 CP    1
3805                 JR    C,LEAVIT       ;LEAVE OR
78                   LD    A,B
2001                 JR    NZ,FILL        ;FILL OR ELSE
08           ROLL    EX    AF,AF'         ;ROLL
12           FILL    LD    (DE),A
7C           LEAVIT  LD    A,H            ;REPEAT UNTIL WHOLE SCREEN
FE58                 CP    58H            ;IS SCROLLED.
38E3                 JR    C,NXTROWS
C9                   RET                  ;RETURN TO BASIC.
                     END
```

41

UP AND DOWN FOR RECTANGLES

UPR and DOWNR are listed seperately because too many POKEs are
required to make converting from one routine to the other
worthwhile during a program. The contents of the last
thirty-two bytes of the printer buffer are used by the
routines, so don't store anything there or use an unterminated
LPRINT command before calling the routines with the usual
LET L = USR ... command.

HEX.	;UPR LENGTH: 108 BYTES		
ED4B245B	START LD	BC,(5B24H)	;C=L1, B=C1
2A265B	LD	HL,(5B26H)	;L=L2, H=C2
7D	LD	A,L	;CHECK FOR ILLEGAL
FE18	CP	18H	;COORDINATES.
D0	RET	NC	
91	SUB	C	
D8	RET	C	
57	LD	D,A	
7C	LD	A,H	
FE20	CP	20H	
D0	RET	NC	
90	SUB	B	
D8	RET	C	
5F	LD	E,A	
1C	INC	E	;E=WIDTH OF RECTANGLE.
D5	PUSH	DE	;D=NUMBER OF LINES-1
79	LD	A,C	;FIND THE ADDRESS OF THE
E618	AND	18H	;TOP-LEFT CORNER (L1,C1).
C640	ADD	A,40H	
67	LD	H,A	
79	LD	A,C	
87	ADD	A,A	
87	ADD	A,A	
87	ADD	A,A	
87	ADD	A,A	
87	ADD	A,A	
80	ADD	A,B	
6F	LD	L,A	
C1	POP	BC	
C5	NXTROWS PUSH	BC	
E5	PUSH	HL	
C5	PUSH	BC	
AF	XOR	A	
11E05B	LD	DE,5BE0H	;STORE THE TOP ROW OF THE
47	LD	B,A	;TOP LINE OF THE RECTANGLE
E5	PUSH	HL	;IN THE PRINTER BUFFER.
EDB0	LDIR		
D1	POP	DE	
C1	POP	BC	
B8	CP	B	;IS THE RECTANGLE ONLY
2816	JR	Z,DONE	;ONE LINE DEEP? IF SO THEN
C5	NXTLINE PUSH	BC	;DON'T SCROLL.
212000	LD	HL,20H	;FIND THE POSITION OF THE
44	LD	B,H	;ROWS IN MEMORY WHICH ARE

42

```
19                 ADD    HL,DE        ;BEING MOVED UP.
7D                 LD     A,L
FE20               CP     20H
3004               JR     NC,NOTTHRD
7C                 LD     A,H
C607               ADD    A,7
67                 LD     H,A
E5        NOTTHRD  PUSH   HL           ;NOW MOVE THE ROWS UP TO
EDB0               LDIR                ;THEIR NEW POSITION, AND...
D1                 POP    DE           ;REPEAT UNTIL ALL OF THE
C1                 POP    BC           ;TOP ROWS OF EACH
10EA               DJNZ   NXTLINE      ;CHARACTER HAVE BEEN
2A325B    DONE     LD     HL,(5B32H)   ;SCROLLED. TEST (23346).
7D                 LD     A,L
FE01               CP     1            ;DECIDE WHETHER TO
380F               JR     C,LEAVIT     ;LEAVE,
2007               JR     NZ,FILL      ;FILL OR
21E05B    ROLL     LD     HL,5BE0H     ;ROLL THE GRAPHICS.
EDB0               LDIR
1806               JR     LEAVIT
41        FILL     LD     B,C          ;FILL THE TOP-ROW OF EACH
7C                 LD     A,H          ;CHARACTER WITH THE DESIRED
12        NXT1     LD     (DE),A       ;PATTERN.
13                 INC    DE
10FC               DJNZ   NXT1
E1        LEAVIT   POP    HL           ;NOW REPEAT WHOLE OPERATION
C1                 POP    BC           ;FOR THE OTHER 7 ROWS OF
24                 INC    H            ;EACH CHARACTER IN THE
7C                 LD     A,H          ;RECTANGLE, AND...
E607               AND    7
20BB               JR     NZ,NXTROWS
C9                 RET                 ;RETURN TO BASIC.
                   END
```

```
HEX.      ;DOWNR LENGTH: 109 BYTES
ED4B245B  START    LD     BC,(5B24H)   ;C=L1, B=C1
2A265B             LD     HL,(5B26H)   ;L=L2, H=C2
7D                 LD     A,L          ;CHECK FOR ILLEGAL
FE18               CP     18H          ;COORDINATES.
D0                 RET    NC
91                 SUB    C
D8                 RET    C
57                 LD     D,A
7C                 LD     A,H
FE20               CP     20H
D0                 RET    NC
90                 SUB    B
D8                 RET    C
5F                 LD     E,A
1C                 INC    E            ;E=WIDTH OF RECTANGLE.
D5                 PUSH   DE           ;D=NUMBER OF LINES-1
7D                 LD     A,L          ;FIND THE ADDRESS OF THE
E618               AND    18H          ;BOTTOM-LEFT CORNER
C640               ADD    A,40H        ;(L2,C1).
```

43

```
67                 LD    H,A
7D                 LD    A,L
87                 ADD   A,A
87                 ADD   A,A
87                 ADD   A,A
87                 ADD   A,A
80                 ADD   A,B
6F                 LD    L,A
C1                 POP   BC
C5     NXTROWS PUSH BC
E5             PUSH  HL
C5             PUSH  BC
AF             XOR   A
11E05B         LD    DE,5BE0H    ;STORE THE TOP ROW OF THE
47             LD    B,A          ;BOTTOM LINE OF THE
E5             PUSH  HL           ;RECTANGLE IN THE PRINTER
EDB0           LDIR               ;BUFFER.
D1             POP   DE
C1             POP   BC
B8             CP    B            ;IS THE RECTANGLE ONLY
2817           JR    Z,DONE       ;ONE LINE DEEP? IF SO THEN
C5     NXTLINE PUSH BC            ;DON'T SCROLL.
21E0FF         LD    HL,0FFE0H    ;FIND THE POSITION OF THE
0600           LD    B,0          ;ROWS IN MEMORY WHICH ARE
19             ADD   HL,DE        ;BEING MOVED DOWN.
7D             LD    A,L
FEE0           CP    0E0H
3804           JR    C,NOTTHRD
7C             LD    A,H
D607           SUB   7
67             LD    H,A
E5     NOTTHRD PUSH HL            ;NOW MOVE THE ROWS UP TO
EDB0           LDIR               ;THEIR NEW POSITION, AND
D1             POP   DE           ;REPEAT UNTIL ALL OF THE
C1             POP   BC           ;TOP ROWS OF EACH
10E9           DJNZ  NXTLINE      ;CHARACTER HAVE BEEN
2A325B DONE    LD    HL,(5B32H)   ;SCROLLED. TEST (23346)
7D             LD    A,L
FE01           CP    1            ;DECIDE WHETHER TO
380F           JR    C,LEAVIT     ;LEAVE,
2007           JR    NZ,FILL      ;FILL OR
21E05B ROLL    LD    HL,5BE0H     ;ROLL THE GRAPHICS.
EDB0           LDIR
1806           JR    LEAVIT
41     FILL    LD    B,C          ;FILL THE TOP-ROW OF EACH
7C             LD    A,H          ;CHARACTER WITH THE
12     NXT1    LD    (DE),A       ;DESIRED PATTERN.
13             INC   DE
10FC           DJNZ  NXT1
E1     LEAVIT  POP   HL           ;NOW REPEAT WHOLE
C1             POP   BC           ;OPERATION FOR THE OTHER
24             INC   H            ;7 ROWS OF EACH CHARACTER
```

```
7C            LD    A,H          ;IN THE RECTANGLE, AND...
E607          AND   7
20BA          JR    NZ,NXTROWS
C9            RET                ;RETURN TO BASIC.
              END
```

UP AND DOWN FOR THE WHOLE SCREEN

The last two routines in this chapter are UPWS and DOWNWS (WS for Whole Screen). The only POKEs, of course, are 23346 and 23347. Both of the routines, like their 'rectangle' counterparts, erase the contents of the last thirty-two bytes of the printer buffer.

```
HEX.          ;UPWS LENGTH: 67 BYTES
210040  START    LD    HL,4000H       ;BEGINNING OF DISPLAY RAM.
11E05B           LD    DE,5BE0H       ;PRINTER BUFFER.
D5      NXSLICE  PUSH  DE
E5               PUSH  HL
3E03             LD    A,3
012000           LD    BC,20H
C5      NXTHIRD  PUSH  BC             ;STORE THE TOP 'SLICE'
E5               PUSH  HL             ;OF THE TOP LINE IN THE
EDB0             LDIR                 ;PRINTER BUFFER.
D1               POP   DE
0EE0             LD    C,0E0H
EDB0             LDIR                 ;NEXT 7 LINES (1-7) UP
0607             LD    B,7            ;INTO THE TOP 7 LINES
                                      ;(0-6). FIND THE FIRST
09               ADD   HL,BC          ;LINE OF THE NEXT THIRD OF
3D               DEC   A              ;THE SCREEN. REPEAT UNTIL
C1               POP   BC             ;ALL OF THE TOP SLICES HAVE
20F0             JR    NZ,NXTHIRD     ;BEEN SCROLLED UP A LINE.
3A325B           LD    A,(5B32H)      ;TEST(23346)
FE01             CP    1              ;DECIDE WHETHER TO ...
3811             JR    C,LEAVIT       ;LEAVE,
2007             JR    NZ,FILL        ;FILL OR
21E05B  ROLL     LD    HL,5BE0H       ;ROLL THE TOP SLICE DOWN
EDB0             LDIR                 ;INTO THE BOTTOM LINE.
1808             JR    LEAVIT
41      FILL     LD    B,C
3A335B           LD    A,(5B33H)      ;(23347) IS PLACED IN THE
12      NXT1     LD    (DE),A         ;BOTTOM LINE OF THE SCREEN.
13               INC   DE
10FC             DJNZ  NXT1
E1      LEAVIT   POP   HL             ;MOVE TO THE SECOND SLICE
D1               POP   DE             ;OF EACH LINE, AND REPEAT
24               INC   H              ;THE WHOLE OPERATION UNTIL
7C               LD    A,H            ;ALL 8 SLICES OF ALL 24
FE48             CP    48H            ;LINES HAVE BEEN SCROLLED.
38C9             JR    C,NXSLICE
EB      CLEANUP  EX    DE,HL          ;CLEAN UP THE PRINTER
73      NXT2     LD    (HL),E         ;BUFFER.
2C               INC   L
20FC             JR    NZ,NXT2
C9               RET                  ;RETURN TO BASIC.
                 END
```

```
                  ;DOWNWS  LENGTH: 69 BYTES
21FF57     START   LD    HL,57FFH        ;END OF DISPLAY RAM.
11FF5B             LD    DE,5BFFH        ;PRINTER BUFFER.
D5         NXSLICE PUSH  DE
E5                 PUSH HL
3E03               LD    A,3
012000             LD    BC,20H
C5         NXTTHRD PUSH  BC              ;STORE THE BOTTOM 'SLICE'
E5                 PUSH  HL              ;OF THE BOTTOM LINE IN THE
EDB8               LDDR                  ;PRINTER BUFFER.
D1                 POP   DE
0EE0               LD    C,0E0H          ;MOVE THE BOTTOM SLICES OF
EDB8               LDDR                  ;THE NEXT 7 LINES (22-16)
06F9               LD    B,0F9H          ;DOWN INTO THE BOTTOM 7
09                 ADD   HL,BC           ;LINES (23-17). FIND THE
                                         ;BOTTOM LINE OF THE NEXT
                                         ;THIRD OF THE SCREEN.
C1                 POP   BC              ;REPEAT UNTIL ALL OF THE
3D                 DEC   A               ;BOTTOM SLICES HAVE BEEN
20F0               JR    NZ,NXTTHRD      ;SCROLLED DOWN A LINE.
3A325B             LD    A,(5B32H)       ;TEST(23346)
FE01               CP    1               ;DECIDE WHETHER TO ...
3811               JR    C,LEAVIT        ;LEAVE,
2007               JR    NZ,FILL         ;FILL OR
21FF5B     ROLL    LD    HL,5BFFH        ;ROLL THE BOTTOM SLICE UP
EDB8               LDDR                  ;INTO THE TOP LINE.
1808               JR    LEAVIT
41         FILL    LD    B,C
3A335B             LD    A,(5B33H)       ;(23347) IS PLACED IN THE
12         NXT1    LD    (DE),A          ;TOP LINE OF THE SCREEN.
1B                 DEC   DE
10FC               DJNZ  NXT1
E1         LEAVIT  POP   HL              ;MOVE ON TO THE
                                         ;PENULTIMATE SLICE OF EACH
D1                 POP   DE              ;LINE AND REPEAT THE WHOLE
25                 DEC   H               ;THE WHOLE OPERATION UNTIL
7C                 LD    A,H             ;ALL 8 SLICES OF ALL 24
FE50               CP    50H             ;LINES HAVE BEEN SCROLLED.
30C9               JR    NC,NXSLICE
AF                 XOR   A               ;CLEAN UP THE PRINTER
0620               LD    B,20H           ;BUFFER.
12         NXT2    LD    (DE),A
1B                 DEC   DE
10FC               DJNZ  NXT2
C9                 RET                   ;RETURN TO BASIC.
                   END
```

DEMONSTRATION PROGRAM - CRISS-CROSS
Here then is the demonstration program as described under
'applications' at the beginning of this chapter.

Notes:
1) The numbers in line 20 are the locations of the four
rectangle routines and will probably be different for you,
depending on where and in what order you store them in memory.

2) The quotes in line 40 contain 5 spaces; those in line 70, one space.
Once the computer has jumbled up the tiles on the puzzle, enter the number on the appropriate cursor key in order to state which way you want the 'hole' in the grid to move. When you have put the tiles back into the right order, see if you can write a BASIC subroutine that makes the computer solve the puzzle, illustrating its moves as its goes.

```
  10 REM CRISS-CROSS © DAVID M.
WEBB 1982
  20 LET UP=65240: LET DOWN=6513
1: LET LEFT=65042: LET RIGHT=649
53
  30 RANDOMIZE
  40 BORDER 6: PAPER 5: CLS : PA
PER 6: FOR A=0 TO 21: PRINT AT A
,0;"     ";AT A,27;"     ";: NEX
T A
  50 PAPER 2
  60 FOR A=0 TO 20
  70 PRINT AT 0,5+A;" ";AT A,26;
" ";AT 21,26-A;" ";AT 21-A,5;" "
;
  80 NEXT A
  90 INK 4
 100 FOR A=8 TO 128 STEP 40
 110 PLOT 48,A: DRAW 159,0: PLOT
48,A+39: DRAW 159,0
 120 PLOT 40+A,8: DRAW 0,159: PL
OT 79+A,8: DRAW 0,159
 130 NEXT A
 140 INK 0: PAPER 5: REM PRINT N
UMBERS
 150 FOR A=0 TO 3: FOR B=0 TO 3
 160 IF A*4+B+1=16 THEN   GO TO 1
90
 170 PRINT AT 3+A*5,8+B*5;A*4+B+
1
 180 NEXT B: NEXT A
 190 INK 0: PAPER 6
 200 PRINT AT 0,0;"Hang"'"on"'"w
hile"'"I mix"'"the"'"tiles"
 210 POKE 23346,1: REM roll
 220 LET X=21: LET Y=16
 230 FOR A=1 TO 300
 240 LET B=INT (RND*4)+5
 250 GO SUB 350
 260 NEXT A
 270 POKE 23333,0: POKE 23335,4:
POKE 23336,2: POKE 23347,0: REM
"FILL" WITH SPACES
 280 FOR A=0 TO 5: POKE 23332,A:
POKE 23334,A
```

47

```
 290 FOR B=O TO 4: LET L=USR LEF
T
 300 PAUSE 5: NEXT B
 310 NEXT A
 320 POKE 23346,1: REM "ROLL"
 330 INPUT "Which way (5/6/7/8)?
";B: IF B<5 OR B>8 THEN  GO TO 3
30
 340 GO SUB 350: GO TO 330
 350 IF B=8 AND X=21 OR B=5 AND
X=6 OR B=7 AND Y=1 OR B=6 AND Y=
16 THEN  RETURN
 360 POKE 23332,Y-5*(B=7): REM L
1
 370 POKE 23333,X-5*(B=5): REM C
1
 380 POKE 23334,Y+4+5*(B=6): REM
L2
 390 POKE 23335,Y+4+5*(B=8): REM
C2
 400 LET Y=Y+5*((B=6)-(B=7))
 410 LET X=X+5*((B=8)-(B=5))
 420 LET U=(LEFT AND B=5)+(RIGHT
AND B=8)+(UP AND B=7)+(DOWN AND
B=6)
 430 FOR Z=1 TO 5: LET L=USR U:
PAUSE 5: NEXT Z
 440 RETURN
```

CHAPTER 7
SCROLLING BY PIXELS

To complete the set of general-purpose scrolling routines in
this book, here are four that allow you to scroll any window on
the screen by just one pixel in any of four directions. This
provides for much smoother animation in games, but I should
warn you that even in machine code, with large areas of the
screen being scrolled, it takes significantly longer to scroll
eight times by one pixel than just once by one cell (eight
pixels).

To use the routines you must first specify a window, unless you
want the routine to default to the entire top 22 lines of the
screen.

To define the window I have used a new system of coordinates.
The columns are still numbered 0-31, but the "rows" or "lines
of pixels" are numbered DOWN the screen from 0 to 191, thus:

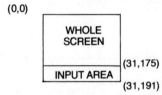

Calling the top-left corner of your rectangle (x1, y1) and the
bottom-right corner (x2, y2), both of which are included in the
rectangle, then your screen should look like this:

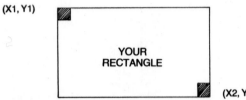

(X1, Y1)

YOUR
RECTANGLE

(X2, Y2)

If T is the start address of your routine, then these are the
POKE addresses for your coordinates. I have prefixed the
routine names with "PW" for "Pixel Window".

Parameter

Routine name				
	X1	X2	Y1	Y2
PW LEFT	T + 41	T + 32	T + 1	T + 23
PW RIGHT	T + 32	T + 37	T + 1	T + 23
PW UP	T + 31	T + 36	T + 1	T + 23
PW DOWN	T + 31	T + 36	T + 27	T + 1

Hence to scroll the top four lines rightwards,

        POKE T + 32, O : POKE T + 37, 31
        POKE T + 1, O : POKE T + 23, 31

The routines offer three different types of scrolling. These
are:
LEAVE — the row or column of pixels exposed by the scroll as it
is;
ROLL — the row or column "pushed out" of the rectangle back
into the opposite end;
FILL — the exposed row or column with something new.

In the case of PW UP and PW DOWN, "Something new" means an
eight-bit binary pattern that will go in the exposed row of
each column, e.g.

        BIN 1111 0000

would provide thick INK and PAPER vertical lines during
repeated scrolling, while

        BIN 0101 0101

would provide a fine "pinstripe" pattern. I'll call this binary
pattern the FILLER byte. To "blank out" the exposed row (i.e.
fill with paper), the filler will be zero. To "black in" the
exposed row (i.e. fill with ink) the filler will be 255 (= BIN
1111 1111).

For PW LEFT and PW RIGHT, you may fill the exposed column with
an INK pixel or a PAPER pixel. The "option number" defining
which option you require is found from this table:

OPTION	PW LEFT, PW RIGHT	PW UP, PW DOWN
0	LEAVE	
1	ROLL	
2	Fill with PAPER	Fill with FILLER byte
3	Fill with INK	

The POKEs are as follows:

> POKE 23361, [OPTION NO.]
> POKE 23362, [Filler byte]

Here is the first one, PW LEFT, with a demonstration program.

```
HEX.              ;PW LEFT  LENGTH: 113 BYTES
            Y1    EQU    0
            Y2    EQU    0AFH
            X1    EQU    0
            X2    EQU    1FH
3E00        START LD     A,Y1      ;LOCATE THE ADDRESS OF
4F                LD     C,A       ;COLUMN 0 IN ROW Y1
E6C0              AND    0C0H
0F                RRCA
0F                RRCA
0F                RRCA
C640              ADD    A,40H
67                LD     H,A
79                LD     A,C
E607              AND    7
84                ADD    A,H
67                LD     H,A
79                LD     A,C
87                ADD    A,A
87                ADD    A,A
E6E0              AND    0E0H
6F                LD     L,A
3EAF              LD     A,Y2      ;CHECK Y2 FOR LEGALITY
FEC0              CP     0C0H      ;THEN SUBTRACT Y1. IF
D0                RET    NC        ;RESULT IS NEGATIVE THEN
91                SUB    C         ;RETURN TO BASIC.
D8                RET    C         ;OTHERWISE Y2-Y1+1=NUMBER
3C                INC    A         ;OF ROWS TO BE SCROLLED.
4F                LD     C,A
061F              LD     B,X2      ;FIND ADDRESS OF (X2,Y1)
7D                LD     A,L
B0                OR     B
6F                LD     L,A
```

```
78              LD      A,B
FE20            CP      20H             ;CHECK X2 AND X1 FOR
D0              RET     NC              ;LEGALITY. X2-X1+1=NUMBER
D600            SUB     X1              ;OF COLUMNS TO BE
D8              RET     C               ;SCROLLED. STORE THIS
3C              INC     A               ;RESULT IN DE.
5F              LD      E,A
1600            LD      D,0
3A415B          LD      A,(5B41H)       ;PUT THE OPTION NUMBER
08              EX      AF,AF'          ;IN A'.
43      NXTROW  LD      B,E             ;SCROLL A ROW LEFTWARDS.
A7              AND     A
CB16    NXTCOL  RL      (HL)
2B              DEC     HL
10FB            DJNZ    NXTCOL
08              EX      AF,AF'          ;DECIDE ON WHETHER TO
19              ADD     HL,DE           ;LEAVE, ROLL OR FILL.
FE01            CP      1
3820            JR      C,LEAVE
2827            JR      Z,ROLL
CBC6            SET     0,(HL)          ;FILL ACCORDING TO BIT
CB47            BIT     0,A             ;0 OF THE OPTION NUMBER.
2002            JR      NZ,SET
CB86            RES     0,(HL)
08      SET     EX      AF,AF'
7C      INIT    LD      A,H             ;LOCATE THE X2
3C              INC     A               ;COLUMN OF THE NEXT
67              LD      H,A             ;ROW DOWN.
E607            AND     7
200A            JR      NZ,OUT
7D              LD      A,L
C620            ADD     A,20H
6F              LD      L,A
3804            JR      C,OUT
7C              LD      A,H
D608            SUB     B
67              LD      H,A
0D      OUT     DEC     C               ;REPEAT PROCEDURE UNTIL
20D4            JR      NZ,NXTROW       ;ALL ROWS OF RECTANGLE ARE
C9              RET                     ;SCROLLED, THEN RETURN TO
08      LEAVE   EX      AF,AF'          ;BASIC.
7E              LD      A,(HL)          ;LEAVE MOVES BIT 1 OF
E602            AND     2               ;COLUMN X2 BACK INTO
1F              RRA                     ;BIT 0.
B6              OR      (HL)
77              LD      (HL),A
18E2            JR      INIT            ;JUMP BACK TO NEXT ROW.
08      ROLL    EX      AF,AF'          ;ROLL THE LEFTMOST BIT OF
3E00            LD      A,0             ;COLUMN X1 OUT OF THE
17              RLA                     ;CARRY AND INTO BIT 0.
B6              OR      (HL)            ;OF COLUMN X2.
77              LD      (HL),A
180A            JR      INIT            ;JUMP BACK TO NEXT ROW.
                END
```

Here is the demonstration; remember to change the start address in line 70 to your value.

```
  10 REM PIXEL WINDOW LEFT-SCROL
L DEMO
  20 REM © DAVID M. WEBB,1983
  30 BRIGHT 1: FLASH 0: INVERSE
0: OVER 0: BORDER 4: PAPER 6: IN
K 4: CLS
  40 REM DEFINE USR GRAPHICS
  50 FOR A=0 TO 7: READ B: POKE
USR "A"+A,B: NEXT A
  60 DATA 0,BIN 10100000,BIN 100
10000,254,8,16,0,0
  70 LET PWL=65000: REM START AD
DRESS
  80 REM DRAW MOUNTAINS
  90 LET Y=28: PLOT 0,Y: FOR A=0
TO 14
 100 LET DY=INT (RND*56)-Y
 110 DRAW 16,DY
 120 LET Y=Y+DY
 130 NEXT A
 140 DRAW 15,28-Y
 150 GO SUB 260: LET A$=CHR$ 144
: INK 2
 160 PRINT AT 10,15;A$;A$;A$;AT
9,14;A$;" ";A$;AT 11,14;A$;" ";A
$;AT 12,13;A$;AT 8,13;A$
 170 PRINT AT 0,1;"RED ARROWS IN
 VIGGEN FORMATION": PLOT 0,167:
DRAW 255,0
 180 REM DEFINE WINDOW
 190 POKE PWL+1,119:      REM Y1
 200 POKE PWL+23,175:     REM Y2
 210 POKE PWL+41,0:       REM X1
 220 POKE PWL+32,31:      REM X2
 230 POKE 23361,1:        REM ROLL
 240 RANDOMIZE USR PWL: GO TO 24
0
 250 REM PAINT-IN MOUNTAINS
 260 FOR A=0 TO 255: LET B=0
 270 IF POINT (A,B) THEN   GO TO
290
 280 LET B=B+1: GO TO 270
 290 PLOT A,0: DRAW 0,B: NEXT A
 300 RETURN
```

PW RIGHT is very similar to PW LEFT. You may like to try altering the demonstration program for PW LEFT so that the planes fly in the opposite direction, or perhaps leave the mountains stationary, define two windows 8 pixels by 32 columns in size and then produce a breath-taking display of two "solo" planes flying from opposite sides of the screen and crossing each other in mid-flight.

Another use for this routine would be to scroll messages across the screen, or maybe to move the landscape in a "Defender" or "Penetrator"-type game.

```
HEX.           ;PW RIGHT LENGTH: 115 BYTES
               Y1      EQU     0
               Y2      EQU     0AFH
               X1      EQU     0
               X2      EQU     01FH
3E00           START   LD      A,Y1        ;LOCATE THE ADDRESS OF
4F                     LD      C,A         ;COLUMN 0 IN ROW Y1.
E6C0                   AND     0C0H
0F                     RRCA
0F                     RRCA
0F                     RRCA
C640                   ADD     A,40H
67                     LD      H,A
79                     LD      A,C
E607                   AND     7
84                     ADD     A,H
67                     LD      H,A
79                     LD      A,C
87                     ADD     A,A
87                     ADD     A,A
E6E0                   AND     0E0H
6F                     LD      L,A
```

```
3EAF          LD      A,Y2        ;CHECK Y2 AND Y1
FEC0          CP      0C0H        ;FOR LEGALITY.
D0            RET     NC
91            SUB     C
D8            RET     C
3C            INC     A           ;Y2-Y1+1=NUMBER OF
4F            LD      C,A         ;ROWS TO BE SCROLLED.
0600          LD      B,X1        ;FIND ADDRESS OF (Y1,X1)
7D            LD      A,L
B0            OR      B
6F            LD      L,A
3E1F          LD      A,X2
FE20          CP      20H         ;CHECK X2 AND X1 FOR
D0            RET     NC          ;LEGALITY. X2-X1+1=NUMBER
90            SUB     B           ;OF COLUMNS TO BE
D8            RET     C           ;SCROLLED. STORE THIS
3C            INC     A           ;RESULT IN DE.
5F            LD      E,A
1600          LD      D,0
3A415B        LD      A,(5B41H)   ;PUT THE OPTION NUMBER
08            EX      AF,AF'      ;IN A'.
43      NXTROW LD      B,E        ;SCROLL A ROW RIGHTWARDS.
A7            AND     A
CB1E    NXTCOL RR      (HL)
23            INC     HL
10FB          DJNZ    NXTCOL
08            EX      AF,AF'      ;DECIDE ON WHETHER TO
A7            AND     A           ;LEAVE, ROLL OR FILL.
ED52          SBC     HL,DE
FE01          CP      1
3820          JR      C,LEAVE
2827          JR      Z,ROLL
CBFE          SET     7,(HL)      ;FILL ACCORDING TO BIT
CB47          BIT     0,A         ;0 OF THE OPTION NUMBER.
2002          JR      NZ,SET
CBBE          RES     7,(HL)
08      SET    EX      AF,AF'
7C      INIT   LD      A,H        ;LOCATE COLUMN X1 OF
3C            INC     A           ;THE NEXT ROW DONE.
67            LD      H,A
E607          AND     7
200A          JR      NZ,OUT
7D            LD      A,L
C620          ADD     A,20H
6F            LD      L,A
3804          JR      C,OUT
7C            LD      A,H
D608          SUB     8
67            LD      H,A
0D      OUT    DEC     C          ;REPEAT UNTIL ALL ROWS OF
20D2          JR      NZ,NXTROW   ;RECTANGLE ARE SCROLLED,
C9            RET                 ;THEN RETURN TO BASIC.
08      LEAVE  EX      AF,AF'     ;LEAVE MOVES BIT 6 OF
7E            LD      A,(HL)      ;COLUMN X1 BACK INTO
E640          AND     40H         ;BIT 7.
```

```
17              RLA
B6              OR    (HL)
77              LD    (HL),A
18E2            JR    INIT      ;JUMP BACK TO NEXT ROW.
08      ROLL    EX    AF,AF'    ;ROLL THE RIGHTMOST BIT OF
3E00            LD    A,0       ;COLUMN X2 OUT OF THE
1F              RRA             ;CARRY AND BACK INTO
B6              OR    (HL)      ;BIT 7 OF COLUMN X1
77              LD    (HL),A
18DA            JR    INIT      ;JUMP BACK TO NEXT ROW.
                END
```

Here is a demonstration program for PW RIGHT.
I have included lines 180 to 210 as an example of how to make
the program "auto-run" on loading. Don't forget to alter the
start address in line 30 and the corresponding values in lines
170 to 210 to suit your own start address.

```
  10 REM PIXEL WINDOW RIGHT-SCRO
LL DEMO
  20 REM © DAVID M. WEBB, 1983
  30 LET PWR=65000: REM START AD
DRESS OF PIXEL WINDOW RIGHT
  40 OVER 1: PAPER 6: INK 2: BOR
DER 1 : CLS
  50 PRINT TAB 9;"OSCILLOSCOPE?"
  60 PLOT 0,87: DRAW 255,0: REM
AXIS
  70 REM DEFINE WINDOW
  80 POKE PWR+1,24:     REM Y1
  90 POKE PWR+23,152:   REM Y2
 100 POKE PWR+32,0:     REM X1
 110 POKE PWR+37,31:    REM X2
 120 POKE 23361,0: REM LEAVE OLD
COLUMN
 130 FOR A=0 TO 252
 140 PLOT 0,87+64*SIN (A*PI/63):
PLOT  OVER 0,0,87
 150 RANDOMIZE USR PWR: NEXT A
 160 POKE 23361,1: REM ROLL
 170 RANDOMIZE USR PWR: GO TO 17
 175 REM
 176 REM
 180 REM I USED THIS TO AUTO LOA
D THE MACHINE CODE......
 190 CLEAR 64999: LOAD "RPIXWIND
OW"CODE 65000,115: RUN
 200 REM ...AND THIS TO SAVE
 210 SAVE "PWR DEMO" LINE 180: S
AVE "RPIXWINDOW"CODE 65000,115
```

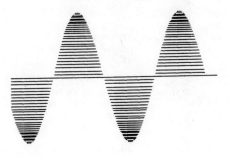

OSCILLOSCOPE?

Now for PW UP, which could be used highly effectively in "launching" a rocket from the bottom of the screen, or perhaps rotating the "fruit" dials in a fruit machine simulation. Two demonstration programs follow.

HEX.	;PW UP	LENGTH: 115 BYTES		
	Y1	EQU	0	
	Y2	EQU	0AFH	
	X1	EQU	0	
	X2	EQU	1FH	
3E00	START	LD	A,Y1	;LOCATE THE ADDRESS OF
4F		LD	C,A	;COLUMN 0 IN ROW Y1.
E6C0		AND	0C0H	
0F		RRCA		
0F		RRCA		
0F		RRCA		
C640		ADD	A,40H	
67		LD	H,A	
79		LD	A,C	
E607		AND	7	
84		ADD	A,H	
67		LD	H,A	
79		LD	A,C	
87		ADD	A,A	
87		ADD	A,A	
E6E0		AND	0E0H	
6F		LD	L,A	
3EAF		LD	A,Y2	;CHECK Y2 AND Y1
FEC0		CP	0C0H	;FOR LEGALITY.
D0		RET	NC	
91		SUB	C	
D8		RET	C	
08		EX	AF,AF'	
0E00		LD	C,X1	;FIND ADDRESS OF (X1,Y1).
7D		LD	A,L	
B1		OR	C	
6F		LD	L,A	
3E1F		LD	A,X2	

57

```
FE20            CP      20H         ;CHECK X2 AND X1 FOR
D0              RET     NC          ;LEGALITY.
91              SUB     C
D8              RET     C
3C              INC     A           ;X2-X1+1=WIDTH OF
4F              LD      C,A         ;RECTANGLE. STORE THIS IN
0600            LD      B,0         ;BC.
C5              PUSH    BC
E5              PUSH    HL
11E05B          LD      DE,5BE0H    ;MOVE THE TOP ROW OF THE
EDB0            LDIR                ;RECTANGLE INTO THE PRINTER
E1              POP     HL          ;BUFFER.
C1              POP     BC
D9              EXX
08              EX      AF,AF'      ;IF THE WINDOW IS ONE
A7              AND     A           ;PIXEL HIGH THEN THERE IS
281E            JR      Z,NOSCROL   ;NOTHING LEFT TO SCROLL.
47              LD      B,A         ;B HOLDS THE NUMBER OF
D9      NXTROW  EXX                 ;ROWS LEFT TO SCROLL.
7C              LD      A,H         ;LOCATE THE COLUMN X1
3C              INC     A           ;OF THE NEXT ROW DOWN.
57              LD      D,A
5D              LD      E,L
E607            AND     7
200A            JR      NZ,OUT
7B              LD      A,E
C620            ADD     A,20H
5F              LD      E,A
3804            JR      C,OUT
7A              LD      A,D
D608            SUB     8
57              LD      D,A
EB      OUT     EX      DE,HL
E5              PUSH    HL          ;MOVE THIS ROW UP ONE
C5              PUSH    BC          ;PIXEL WITH A BLOCK-SHIFT
EDB0            LDIR                ;INSTRUCTION.
C1              POP     BC
E1              POP     HL
D9              EXX                 ;REPEAT UNTIL ALL ROWS HAVE
10E3            DJNZ    NXTROW      ;BEEN SCROLLED.
D9      NOSCROL EXX
3A415B          LD      A,(5B41H)   ;DECIDE WHETHER TO FILL,
FE01            CP      1           ;ROLL OR LEAVE THE BOTTOM
D8              RET     C           ;ROW. IF THE LATTER, THEN
2007            JR      NZ,FILL     ;RETURN TO BASIC.
11E05B          LD      DE,5BE0H    ;ROLL THE ROW STORED IN THE
EB              EX      DE,HL       ;PRINTER BUFFER INTO THE
EDB0            LDIR                ;BOTTOM ROW.
C9              RET                 ;RETURN TO BASIC.
3A425B  FILL    LD      A,(5B42H)   ;FILL THE BOTTOM ROW WITH
41              LD      B,C         ;THE FILLER BYTE.
77      NXTFILL LD      (HL),A
23              INC     HL
10FC            DJNZ    NXTFILL
C9              RET                 ;RETURN TO BASIC.
                END
```

The first demonstration is a program that simply lets you "play around" with the size of a window and the type of scrolling, which will then take effect on a listing of the program itself. Line 90 forms an infinite loop, so to try a new window or setting BREAK out and re-RUN the program. You should alter the start address in line 30, and the corresponding values in the optional "auto-load" line, 100.

```
  10 REM UPWARDS PIXEL WINDOW-SC
ROLL DEMONSTRATION
  20 REM © DAVID M. WEBB, 1983
  30 LET X=65000: REM *** START
ADDRESS ***
  40 INPUT "X1 ";X1,"X2 ";X2,"Y1
";Y1,"Y2 ";Y2,"CONTROL ";C
  50 IF C=2 THEN  INPUT "FILLER
";F: POKE 23362,F
  60 POKE 23361,C: POKE X+1,Y1:
POKE X+23,Y2: POKE X+31,X1: POKE
 X+36,X2
  70 BORDER 3: PAPER 6: INK 2: C
LS : LIST 50: LIST 50
  80 REM
  90 RANDOMIZE USR X: GO TO 90
 100 CLEAR 64999: LOAD "UPIXWIND
OW"CODE 65000: RUN
```

The second demonstration program for PW UP is somewhat more spectacular, and shows a "number-dial" pixel-scrolling past a window in the centre of the screen, rather like a fruit machine dial past its display window.

I have used the trick of making INK and PAPER the same colour over the part of the screen (line 130) just below the display window, and then invisibly printing a number there after every eight pixel-scrolls, ready to be moved up into the display window.

Please remember, as always, to alter the start address in line 50 to your value. The scrolling may be speeded up by removing the PAUSE in line 130.

```
  10 REM UPWARDS PIXEL WINDOW-SC
ROLL DEMONSTRATION (2)
  20 REM © DAVID M. WEBB, 1983
  30 OVER 0: INVERSE 0: FLASH 0:
 BORDER 6: PAPER 6: CLS
  40 PRINT AT 11,15; INK 0; PAPE
R 7;"  "
  50 LET UP=65000: REM   ***START
ADDRESS ***
  60 POKE UP+1,11*8:      REM Y1
  70 POKE UP+23,13*8:     REM Y2
```

```
  80 POKE UP+31,15:        REM X1
  90 POKE UP+36,16:        REM X2
 100 POKE 23361,0:         REM LEA
VE
 110 LET C=0: REM COUNTER
 120 PLOT 112,96: DRAW 31,0: DRA
W 0,-26: DRAW -31,0: DRAW 0,26
 130 PRINT  INK 6; PAPER 6;AT 12
,15;C: FOR A=0 TO 6: PAUSE 1: RA
NDOMIZE USR UP: NEXT A: LET C=C+
1: IF C=100 THEN  LET C=0
 140 RANDOMIZE USR UP: GO TO 130
```

I come now to the logical conclusion of this chapter, the routine PW DOWN. The two demonstration programs above may be easily adapted, using the information at the start of this chapter, to work with PW DOWN.

```
HEX.          ;PW DOWN LENGTH: 116 BYTES
              Y1    EQU    0
              Y2    EQU    0AFH
              X1    EQU    0
              X2    EQU    1FH
              ORG    8000H
3EAF   START  LD     A,Y2          ;LOCATE THE ADDRESS OF
FEC0          CP     0C0H          ;COLUMN 0 IN ROW Y2.
D0            RET    NC            ;CHECK Y2 FOR LEGALITY.
4F            LD     C,A
E6C0          AND    0C0H
0F            RRCA
0F            RRCA
0F            RRCA
C640          ADD    A,40H
67            LD     H,A
79            LD     A,C
E607          AND    7
84            ADD    A,H
67            LD     H,A
79            LD     A,C
87            ADD    A,A
87            ADD    A,A
E6E0          AND    0E0H
6F            LD     L,A
79            LD     A,C
D600          SUB    Y1            ;CHECK Y1 FOR LEGALITY.
D8            RET    C
08            EX     AF,AF'
0E00          LD     C,X1          ;FIND ADDRESS OF (X1,Y2).
7D            LD     A,L
B1            OR     C
6F            LD     L,A
3E1F          LD     A,X2
FE20          CP     20H           ;CHECK X2 AND X1 FOR
D0            RET    NC            ;LEGALITY.
91            SUB    C
```

60

```
D8                 RET    C
3C                 INC    A          ;X2-X1+1=WIDTH OF
4F                 LD     C,A        ;RECTANGLE. STORE THIS
0600               LD     B,0        ;IN BC.
C5                 PUSH   BC
E5                 PUSH   HL
11E05B             LD     DE,5BE0H   ;MOVE THE BOTTOM ROW OF
EDB0               LDIR              ;THE RECTANGLE INTO THE
E1                 POP    HL         ;PRINTER BUFFER.
C1                 POP    BC
D9                 EXX
08                 EX     AF,AF'     ;IF THE WINDOW IS ONE
A7                 AND    A          ;PIXEL HIGH THEN THERE IS
28 1F              JR     Z,NOSCROL  ;NOTHING LEFT TO SCROLL.
47                 LD     B,A        ;B HOLDS THE NUMBER OF
D9        NXTROW   EXX               ;ROWS LEFT TO SCROLL.
7C                 LD     A,H        ;LOCATE COLUMN X1 OF THE
3D                 DEC    A          ;NEXT ROW UP.
57                 LD     D,A
5D                 LD     E,L
2F                 CPL
E607               AND    7
200A               JR     NZ,OUT
7B                 LD     A,E
D620               SUB    20H
5F                 LD     E,A
3804               JR     C,OUT
7A                 LD     A,D
C608               ADD    A,8
57                 LD     D,A
EB        OUT      EX     DE,HL
E5                 PUSH   HL         ;MOVE THIS ROW DOWN ONE
C5                 PUSH   BC         ;PIXEL WITH A BLOCK-SHIFT
EDB0               LDIR              ;INSTRUCTION.
C1                 POP    BC
E1                 POP    HL
D9                 EXX               ;REPEAT UNTIL THE WINDOW
10E2               DJNZ   NXTROW     ;HAS BEEN SCROLLED.
D9        NOSCROL  EXX
3A415B             LD     A,(5B41H)  ;DECIDE WHETHER TO FILL,
FE01               CP     1          ;ROLL OR LEAVE THE TOP
D8                 RET    C          ;ROW OF THE WINDOW. IF THE
2007               JR     NZ,FILL    ;LATTER, THEN RETURN TO
11E05B             LD     DE,5BE0H   ;BASIC. ROLL THE ROW OUT
EB                 EX     DE,HL      ;OF THE PRINTER BUFFER
EDB0               LDIR              ;INTO THE TOP ROW, THEN
C9                 RET               ;RETURN TO BASIC.
3A425B    FILL     LD     A,(5B42H)  ;FILL THE TOP ROW WITH
41                 LD     B,C        ;THE FILLER BYTE.
77        NXTFILL  LD     (HL),A
23                 INC    HL
10FC               DJNZ   NXTFILL
C9                 RET               ;RETURN TO BASIC.
                   END
```

CHAPTER 8
CARPET-ROLL CLS

Here are two handy, novelty screen-clearing routines that can
be used as direct substitutes for CLS.

Imagine, if you will, that the text and graphics on your screen
are printed on a flat carpet, that the carpet is see-through,
and that underneath it is a white lino (a blank screen). These
routines take the carpet by one of the vertical edges and
"roll" it up into a 1-column by 24-line roll, revealing as they
go the "lino" or blank screen underneath. The "roll" of text
makes its way from one side of the screen to the other,
becoming visually darker as it "picks up" more text and
graphics, until it eventually "falls off" the far edge of the
screen, leaving a blank screen. The colour attributes are also
altered according to the current INK, PAPER and BORDER colours
as each column is cleared.

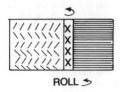

ROLL ⇒

The first routine, RIGHT PEEL-OFF, clears the screen from left
to right. You can vary the speed of the clear by means of a

simple POKE, which controls the length of the PAUSE made after each column of the screen has been cleared.

If S = [start address], then
POKE S + 5, [length of pause]

Note that a value of O corresponds to a PAUSE of 256. To remove the PAUSE altogether, POKE S + 6, O. To get it back, POKE S + 6, 118.

Here is RIGHT PEEL-OFF, followed by a demonstration program.

Call the routine with the usual

LET A = USR [start address]

```
HEX.        ;RIGHT PEEL-OFF LENGTH: 78 BYTES
            ATTRP    EQU    5C8DH
            BORDCR   EQU    5C48H
2E00        START    LD     L,0          ;HL=TOP-LEFT CORNER OF
2640        NXTCOL   LD     H,40H        ;SCREEN.
0603                 LD     B,3          ;DO A PAUSE
76          PAUSE    HALT
10FD                 DJNZ   PAUSE
4E          NXTBYTE  LD     C,(HL)       ;BLANK OUT THE CURRENT
3600                 LD     (HL),0       ;COLUMN,...
0608                 LD     B,8
CB19        NXTROT   RR     C            ;...PRODUCE ITS MIRROR
17                   RLA                 ;IMAGE...
10FB                 DJNZ   NXTROT
23                   INC    HL           ;AND OR IT WITH THE
B6                   OR     (HL)         ;NEXT COLUMN TO THE RIGHT.
77                   LD     (HL),A
111F00               LD     DE,001FH     ;MOVE ONTO THE NEXT
19                   ADD    HL,DE        ;ROW OF THE SCREEN.
7C                   LD     A,H          ;ARE WE AT THE BOTTOM?
FE58                 CP     58H
20EA                 JR     NZ,NXTBYTE   ;IF NOT THEN REPEAT THE
13                   INC    DE           ;PROCESS.
0616                 LD     B,16H        ;NOW TAKE THE INK
3A8D5C               LD     A,(ATTRP)    ;AND PAPER ETC., AND
77          NXTOP    LD     (HL),A       ;FILL OUT THE CURRENT
19                   ADD    HL,DE        ;COLUMN'S ATTRIBUTES.
10FC                 DJNZ   NXTOP
3A845C               LD     A,(BORDCR)   ;USE THE BORDER COLOR
77                   LD     (HL),A       ;FOR THE BOTTOM TWO
19                   ADD    HL,DE        ;LINES.
77                   LD     (HL),A
19                   ADD    HL,DE
2C                   INC    L            ;HAVE WE REACHED THE LAST
7D                   LD     A,L          ;COLUMN OF THE SCREEN? IF
FE1F                 CP     1FH          ;NOT THEN ROLL UP THE
20CC                 JR     NZ,NXTCOL    ;NEXT COLUMN.
2640                 LD     H,40H        ;BLANK OUT THE LAST
06C0                 LD     B,0C0H       ;COLUMN,...
```

```
72         NXTROW  LD    (HL),D
19                 ADD   HL,DE
10FC               DJNZ  NXTROW
3A805C             LD    A,(ATTRP)    ;FILL IN ITS ATTRIBUTES...
0616               LD    B,16H
77         NXTOP2  LD    (HL),A
19                 ADD   HL,DE
10FC               DJNZ  NXTOP2
3A845C             LD    A,(BORDCR)
77                 LD    (HL),A
19                 ADD   HL,DE
77                 LD    (HL),A
C9                 RET                ;AND RETURN TO BASIC.
                   END
```

Note that as it stands, there is a PAUSE of 3 after clearing
columns. This following demonstration uses a PAUSE of 20, and
makes use of the fact that the routine also affects the
attributes. It does this by changing the PAPER colour just
before the routine is called, so that as the screen is "rolled
back" it reveals a differently coloured blank screen
underneath.

```
   10 REM RIGHT PEEL-OFF DEMO
   20 LET CLSB=65200: REM ENTER Y
OUR START ADDRESS
   30 PAPER 6: INK 2: CLS
   40 CIRCLE 128,87,87: PAPER 4:
REM PAPER ALTERED
   50 POKE CLSB+5,20: REM SET SPE
ED
   60 RANDOMIZE USR CLSB
```

Now I couldn't really resist giving you the luxurious choice of
a carpet-roll CLS in two directions, so here for all
left-handed or ambidextrous readers is "LEFT PEEL-OFF". All of
the BASIC programming is the same as for RIGHT PEEL-OFF, and
the same demonstration program will work (you can adjust the
REM in line 10 if you wish!), so I'll just leave you with the
code:

```
HEX.        ;LEFT PEEL-OFF  LENGTH: 75 BYTES
            ATTRP   EQU   5C8DH
            BORDCR  EQU   5C48H
2E1F        START   LD    L,1FH        ;HL=TOP-LEFT CORNER OF
2640        NXTCOL  LD    H,40H        ;SCREEN.
0603                LD    B,3          ;DO A PAUSE
76          PAUSE   HALT
10FD                DJNZ  PAUSE
4E          NXTBYTE LD    C,(HL)       ;BLANK OUT THE CURRENT
3600                LD    (HL),0       ;COLUMN,...
0608                LD    B,8
CB19        NXTROT  RR    C            ;...PRODUCE ITS MIRROR
17                  RLA                ;IMAGE...
10FB                DJNZ  NXTROT
```

```
2B                DEC    HL              ;AND OR IT WITH THE
B6                OR     (HL)            ;NEXT COLUMN TO THE LEFT.
77                LD     (HL),A
112100            LD     DE,0021H        ;MOVE ONTO THE NEXT
19                ADD    HL,DE           ;ROW OF THE SCREEN.
7C                LD     A,H             ;ARE WE AT THE BOTTOM?
FE58              CP     58H
20EA              JR     NZ,NXTBYTE      ;IF NOT THEN REPEAT THE
1B                DEC    DE              ;PROCESS.
0616              LD     B,16H           ;NOW TAKE THE INK
3A8D5C            LD     A,(ATTRP)       ;AND PAPER ETC., AND
77       NXTOP    LD     (HL),A          ;FILL OUT THE CURRENT
19                ADD    HL,DE           ;COLUMN'S ATTRIBUTES.
10FC              DJNZ   NXTOP
3A485C            LD     A,(BORDCR)      ;USE THE BORDER COLOR
77                LD     (HL),A          ;FOR THE BOTTOM TWO
19                ADD    HL,DE           ;LINES.
77                LD     (HL),A
19                ADD    HL,DE           ;HAVE WE REACHED THE LEFT-MOST COLUMN?
2D                DEC    L               ;IF NOT THEN
20CF              JR     NZ,NXTCOL       ;NEXT COLUMN
2640              LD     H,40H           ;BLANK OUT THE LAST
06C0              LD     B,0C0H          ;COLUMN,...
72       NXTROW   LD     (HL),D
19                ADD    HL,DE
10FC              DJNZ   NXTROW
3A8D5C            LD     A,(ATTRP)       ;FILL IN ITS ATTRIBUTES...
0616              LD     B,16H
77       NXTOP2   LD     (HL),A
19                ADD    HL,DE
10FC              DJNZ   NXTOP2
3A485C            LD     A,(BORDCR)
77                LD     (HL),A
19                ADD    HL,DE
77                LD     (HL),A
C9                RET                    ;AND RETURN TO BASIC.
                  END
```

CHAPTER 9
MIRRORED CHARACTERS

Here is an amusing little routine whose sole effect is to reflect each character on the screen in an imaginary vertical axis dissecting each character cell. This gives the effect of 'mirror writing', and since the routine provides a reflection, the operation is self-inverse, i.e. calling the routine again will bring your characters back to normal.

The routine will also 'reflect' any graphics etc. that happen to be on the screen: this in itself could be used to produce some interesting kaleidoscopic effects.

Here is the code:

```
HEX.        ;MIRROR1  LENGTH: 19 BYTES
210040    START   LD    HL,4000H    ;START OF SCREEN.
4E        NXTCELL LD    C,(HL)      ;TAKE A ROW.
0608              LD    B,8         ;B COUNTS ROTATIONS.
CB11      NXTRTTN RL    C           ;MOVE LEFT-MOST BIT
1F                RRA               ;INTO CARRY AND THEN INTO A.
10FB              DJNZ  NXTRTTN     ;NEXT BIT
77                LD    (HL),A      ;RESTORE THE ROW.
23                INC   HL          ;NEXT BYTE OF MEMORY.
7C                LD    A,H         ;HAVE WE REACHED THE
FE58              CP    58H         ;ATTRIBUTE AREA?
20F1              JR    NZ,NXTCELL  ;IF NOT THEN CARRY ON,
C9                RET               ;ELSE RETURN TO BASIC.
                  END
```

To use the routine, just type

RANDOMIZE USR (start address)

Here is a BASIC program to demonstrate the routine, along with
a sample output.

```
  5 REM MIRROR DEMO
  6 REM © D.M. WEBB
 10 FOR a=0 TO 7: READ b: POKE
USR "a"+a,b: NEXT a
 20 DATA 60,126,90,126,126,66,6
6,132
 30 FOR a=0 TO 10: FOR b=0 TO 1
5: PRINT "A ";: REM GRAPHIC A
 40 NEXT b: PRINT ''
 50 NEXT a
 60 PRINT AT 10,5;"SPECTRUM SUP
ERCHARGED"
 70 PLOT 40,84: DRAW 167,0: PLO
T 40,100: DRAW 167,0
 80 RANDOMIZE USR 65000: GO TO
80
```

You can alter the routine to work on various thirds of the
screen. Let's take X as the start address, then the alterations
are as follows:

AREA AFFECTED	POKE X + 2,	POKE X + 15,
Whole screen	64	88
Top 1/3	64	72
Middle 1/3	72	80
Bottom 1/3	80	88
Top 2/3	64	80
Bottom 2/3	72	88

You might not always want to work on the whole screen or large
blocks of it, so I have also included a routine which will

reflect any number of consecutive user-definable graphics
characters.

To use this routine, we must start by giving each graphic
character a number. To make it easy, I've used A = 1, B = 2 and
U = 21. A table of the alphabet may be useful:

A - 1	F - 6	K - 11	P - 16	U - 21
B - 2	G - 7	L - 12	Q - 17	
C - 3	H - 8	M - 13	R - 18	
D - 4	I - 9	N - 14	S - 19	
E - 5	J - 10	O - 15	T - 20	

If X is the start address, then POKE (X + 4) with the number of
the first character to be reflected, and POKE (X + 14) with the
number of characters to be reflected. As standard the routine
will reflect all of the UDG characters, and here it is:

```
HEX.        ;MIRROR2  LENGTH: 33 BYTES
        N1      EQU     1
        N2      EQU     15H
2A7B5C  START   LD      HL,(5C7BH)      ;START OF THE UDG AREA.
3E01            LD      A,N1            ;CODE OF THE FIRST
3D              DEC     A               ;CHARACTER.
87              ADD     A,A             ;MULTIPLY BY 8.
87              ADD     A,A
87              ADD     A,A
5F              LD      E,A             ;ADD THE RESULT TO
1600            LD      D,0             ;THE UDG BASE.
19              ADD     HL,DE
3E15            LD      A,N2            ;THE NUMBER OF CHARACTERS
87              ADD     A,A             ;IS MULTIPLIED BY
87              ADD     A,A             ;8 TO GIVE THE NUMBER
87              ADD     A,A             ;OF BYTES.
4F              LD      C,A
0608    NXTROW  LD      B,8             ;B COUNTS THE BITS.
5E              LD      E,(HL)          ;REFLECT ONE BIT.
CB13    NXTBIT  RL      E
1F              RRA
10FB            DJNZ    NXTBIT          ;...EIGHT TIMES.
77              LD      (HL),A          ;RESTORE THE BYTE.
23              INC     HL              ;ON TO THE NEXT ROW
0D              DEC     C               ;UNTIL ALL IS DONE, THEN
20F3            JR      NZ,NXTROW
C9              RET                     ;RETURN TO BASIC.
                END
```

CHAPTER 10
MORE SPECTACULAR WAYS TO CLEAR THE SCREEN

In chapter eight I presented a new way of clearing the screen,
the 'carpet-roll' method. Here are two more techniques.
The first I have called "shifting" for want of a better word.
Every byte of the display file represents a row of eight
pixels. What the routine does is to shift those pixels along
by one pixel to the right. The leftmost pixel is replaced by a
PAPER pixel and the rightmost is lost. This process is
repeated eight times in quick succession, so, that the
resultant effect is a blank screen. The attributes file is then
filled out in the same way as for the CLS command.
As I said, the direction of this shift is to the right. For
slightly different effect (you guessed it, a shift to the left),
if X is the start address,

> POKE X + 9,38 .

To restore the routine to its original form,

> POKE X + 9,62 .

As usual, the routine can be called with the command

> LET A=USR X   .

```
HEX.          ;RIGHTSHIFT CLS    LENGTH : 40 BYTES
1608                LD      D,08H           ;FOR 8 BITS...
210040      NXTSHFT LD      HL,4000H        ;HL=START OF DISPLAY
011800              LD      BC,0018H        ;FILE.
CB3E        NXT     SRL     (HL)            ;SHIFT THE BYTE
23                  INC     HL
10FB                DJNZ    NXT             ;REPEAT 6143 TIMES
0D                  DEC     C
20F8                JR      NZ,NXT
15                  DEC     D               ;NEXT BIT
```

```
20EF            JR      NZ,NXTSHFT
3A8D5C          LD      A,(5CBDH)       ;TAKE S.V. ATTR P
77              LD      (HL),A          ;FILL THE TOP 22 LINES
54              LD      D,H             ;WITH IT
5D              LD      E,L
13              INC     DE
01C002          LD      BC,02C0H
EDB0            LDIR
3A485C          LD      A,(5C48H)       ;TAKE THE BORDER COLOUR
77              LD      (HL),A          ;FILL THE BOTTOM 2
0E3F            LD      C,3FH           ;LINES WITH IT
EDB0            LDIR
C9              RET                     ;RETURN TO BASIC
                END
```

The second new method for screen-clearing is called 'fade-out'
by virtue of its effect. No POKES are required and the result
is highly satisfying.

```
HEX.            ;FADEOUT CLS    LENGTH : 47 BYTES
11FE08              LD      DE,08FEH        ;D COUNTS THE BITS
7B          NXTFADE LD      A,E             ;E IS A ROTATING MASK
07              RLCA                        ;WITH ONE BIT RESET
07              RLCA
07              RLCA
5F              LD      E,A
210040          LD      HL,4000H        ;HL=START OF DISPLAY FILE
011800          LD      BC,0018H
7E          NXT LD      A,(HL)          ;TAKE A BYTE
A3              AND     E               ;AND THE MASK
77              LD      (HL),A          ;REPLACE THE BYTE
23              INC     HL
10FA            DJNZ    NXT             ;REPEAT 6143 TIMES
0D              DEC     C
20F7            JR      NZ,NXT
15              DEC     D               ;NEXT BIT
20E9            JR      NZ,NXTFADE      ;TAKE SYSTEM VARIABLE
3A8D5C          LD      A,(5C8DH)       ;ATTR P
77              LD      (HL),A          ;FILL THE TOP 22 LINES
54              LD      D,H             ;WITH IT
5D              LD      E,L
13              INC     DE
01C002          LD      BC,02C0H
EDB0            LDIR
3A485C          LD      A,(5C48H)       ;TAKE THE BORDER COLOUR
77              LD      (HL),A          ;FILL THE BOTTOM TWO
0E3F            LD      C,3FH           ;LINES WITH IT
EDB0            LDIR
C9              RET                     ;RETURN TO BASIC
                END
```

A COMPLETE AND DETAILED BREAKDOWN OF USEFUL SYSTEM VARIABLES

CHAPTER 11
SYSTEM VARIABLES AND THE KEYBOARD

Between the area in the RAM of the Spectrum which is used to store the screen contents and that which is used to store your BASIC program is a section of memory called the SYSTEM VARIABLES area. It is here that the computer makes its 'notes for future reference' such as what colour the screen border is, which line of your program it is working on and which key is being pressed.

In this section I will explain how you can use the system variables to your advantage – and which ones to avoid! A full list of the system variables and their addresses can be found in Chapter 25 of the Spectrum Manual, here I shall elaborate on some of the descriptions to be found therein.

CONCERNING THE KEYBOARD

1. Address 23556 will hold either

a) 255 if no key is being pressed; or
b) The CODE of the character printed in white on the left–hand side of the key being pressed.

In the latter case the CODE can be thought of as that of the character that INKEY$ would produce if the CAPS LOCK were on and the key concerned were being pressed on its own.

This property can be used to advantage when using INKEY$ in your program. Enter this program and see what effect CAPS SHIFT or SYMBOL SHIFT has when pressed with another key:

```
10 REM To see how SHIFTS affect INKEY$
20 PRINT AT 0,0; INKEY$; "        ": REM
   4 spaces
30 GOTO 20
```

As you can see, the character produced depends not only on
which key is being pressed but also on whether any SHIFT key is
pressed. CAPS LOCK will also change the output. This leads to
complicated lines when using INKEY$. E.g. (after a game)...

```
1000 PRINT "Do you want another game? (Y/N)":
     PAUSE 0:
         IF INKEY$ = "Y" or INKEY$ = "y" or
         INKEY$ = "AND" THEN RUN
1010 STOP
```

We can get round this awkwardness by PEEKing address 23556. Try
this program.

```
10 REM Tidier INKEY$
20 PRINT AT 0, 0; CHR$ PEEK 23556; "      ";
30 GOTO 20.
```

You will find that whatever shift key is pressed, the character
produced is that which appears on the left-hand side of the
other key being pressed. Hence the solution to the above
problem is:

```
1000 PRINT "Do you want another game (Y/N)?"
     : PAUSE 0:
     IF CHR$ PEEK 23556 = "Y" THEN RUN
1020 STOP.
```

There is one more invaluable benefit to be had from this
technique; if more than one key on the board is pressed then
CHR$ PEEK 23556 produces the character of the first key to make
contact, rather than nothing, as in the case of INKEY$. This
can be used to improve game control: so that if you accidentally
press another key whilst moving your LASER-base out of the way
of a bomb then you will survive to fight another battle, rather
than stopping dead (pun evident).

If you intend to use this idea a lot in your program, then it
might be as well to start off with

```
10 LET KEY = 23556
```

so that in future you will only need

```
IF CHR$ PEEK KEY = ...   THEN ...
```

Incidentally, this saves a small amount of memory (both yours
and the machine's!).

2. LAST K: ADDRESS 23560

PEEKing this address will produce the CODE of the last key that
was pressed, whether or not you are still pressing it. As in

the case of address 23556, if more than one key is being
pressed then the CODE of the first key to be pressed takes
precedence. It is worth noting (perhaps) that although CAPS
SHIFT or SYMBOL SHIFT on its own does not affect INKEY$ or the
contents of 23560, together they produce CODE 14, which is
normally used to signify a number in the Spectrum BASIC
listing. These two keys affect the contents of location 23556
in the same way.

There are four other key combinations which produce values for
PEEK 23560 and CODE INKEY$ which do not appear in the Spectrum
Manual. These are as follows:

Keys normally used to produce ...	Value of CODE INKEY$
GRAPHICS (CAPS SHIFT & 9)	15
TRUE VIDEO (CAPS SHIFT & 3)	4
INV VIDEO (CAPS SHIFT & 4)	5
CAPS LOCK (CAPS SHIFT & 2)	6

3. REPDEL

This location address 23561, holds the time that a key must be
held down before it begins to repeat. The time is measured in
50th of a second in Britain, 60th of a second in North America:
these intervals correspond to the time taken for one cycle of
mains current in the respective areas. REPDEL is initially set
at 35, but can be altered by POKEing 23561 with any integer
from 0 to 255. Note that the Spectrum takes the value of
REPDEL, decrements it and then checks to see whether zero has
been reached, so that POKEing REPDEL with zero will result in a
PAUSE of 256 rather than zero before the key repeats.

4. REPPER

Located at 23562, this system variable works in the same
fashion as REPDEL and controls the delay between successive
repeats of a key once a key has begun to repeat. Note again that
a value of 0 represents a PAUSE of 256 rather than zero. Some
idea of the potential speed of key entry can be attained by
POKEing REPDEL and REPPER with a value of one. This is best
attempted only in a program, since it is almost impossible to
type in the commands necessary to restore the variables to
sensible values once they have been reduced to such a level!

Try this program:

```
   10 REM Changing REPPER and REP
DEL
   20 LET A=PEEK 23561: LET B=PEE
K 23562
   30 INPUT "Change REPPER to?";r
epper,"Change REPDEL to?";repdel
   40 POKE 23561,repdel: POKE 235
62,repper
   50 INPUT "Try this , input spe
ed";A$
```

```
60 POKE 23561,A: POKE 23562,B
70 PRINT "Values used:": PRINT
: PRINT "REPDEL=";repdel,"REPPE
R=";repper
80 INPUT "Another combination
(y/n)?";A$
90 IF A$="y" THEN  GO TO 30
```

Using the program you will be able to select the combination of
REPPER and REPDEL that suits you best. If you intend to do a
lot of typing, it may well be worth POKEing in these values
before you start. Note however, that NEW resets REPDEL to 35
and REPPER to its usual value of 5.

5. RASP

Location 23608 holds the length of that grating warning buzz
that occurs when your INPUT has spilled off the bottom of the
screen and you continue to try to enter the line. It may be of
interest that although the buzz occurs on every keystroke after
a screen overflow, the line is still being entered, and
(providing the syntax of the BASIC line is correct) the string
or BASIC line will still be acceptable to the Spectrum.

The value of RASP can be varied, from its initial 64 at power
up, between 0 and 255, and each increment of the value
corresponds to about one 65th of a second in the duration of
the tone. Thus one way of entering a very large REM statement
(in which to store machine code) would be to POKE RASP to its
lowest value of 0 (to speed up proceedings) and then to enter
the line all in one go. The following system variable should
also be set to zero for speed:

6. PIP

This is the length of the sound emitted from the Spectrum
(apart from the usual buzz) every time a key is pressed during
an INPUT or while in direct command of the computer. Initially
set at zero at power up, address 23609 can be POKEd to change
PIP up to its maximum of 255, which corresponds to about one
3rd of a second. Hence each increment corresponds to about one
765th of a second.

Note that neither RASP or PIP are affected by the NEW command.
```
```

CHAPTER 12
FORCING ERROR REPORTS

As you know, whenever you do something in BASIC that your
Spectrum does not like, it grinds to a halt and gives you one
of those annoying but none-the-less very helpful messages.
These are called 'Error Reports' and a list of them can be
found in appendix B, page 189 of the Spectrum Manual.

Whenever the Spectrum decides that it is about to deliver unto
you an error message, it gives the number or letter preceding
the message (e.g. R in "R Tape loading error") a value, and
stores this value as the system variable 'ERR NR' (for ERRor
NumbeR).

ERR NR can be found in location 23610, and the value for each
error report is decided as follows:

REPORT CODE	ERRNR Value
0 to 9	Subtract 1 from report code (0 becomes 255)
A to R	Add 8 to the position of the report code in the alphabet.

Hence code 9 has value 8, A has value 9, B has value 10 and so
on.

There are essentially two ways to force the computer to stop
with any required report code (apart from trying to make the
required mistake!)

The first method is totally in BASIC. You simply POKE the

appropriate value into ERR NR for the report required, and then make sure the program ends without producing any more reports (since these would alter the value of ERR NR). Perhaps the easiest way to do this is as follows:

```
(any line) POKE 23610, [appropriate value] :
           GOTO 9999
9999 REM
```

Note that the line 9999 is just a 'dummy' line whose sole purpose is to ensure that 'GOTO 9999' does not produce the report "0 OK". There is one small snag, however; the line number and statement number in the report will be "9999:1". To get around this, you can make use of the system variables PPC (locations 23621 and 23622) and SUBPPC (23623). PPC holds the current line number and SUBPPC the current statement number. Hence in the above example we can produce the exact line and statement numbers required in the report code, by POKEing in appropriate values of PPC and SUBPPC.

If L is the line number required, change line 9999 from

```
9999 REM
```

to

```
9999 POKE 23621, L - 256 * INT(L / 256):
     POKE 23622, INT(L / 256):
     POKE 23623, [statement number]
```

N.B. To cause a "0 OK" report on the current line, insert the command

```
POKE 23611, PEEK 23611 -128.
```

The second method involves one of the shortest pieces of machine code you are ever likely to come across. It goes like this:

Comment	Mnemonic	Hex
Call error routine	RST 8	CF
Data byte = value of ERRNR	DEFB	(FF)

This is so short that it can be POKEd into the two spare bytes to be found near the end of the system variables. They are locations 23728 and 23729.

Hence to force an error report at any time in a program, use the line:

```
(Line L)    POKE 23728, 207 : POKE 23729, [ appropriate value
            of ERRNR] : RANDOMIZE USR 23728
```

The line number in the report will be L, the statement number will be three and the program will stop immediately.

NEWPPC, NSPPC

I have already mentioned PPC and SUBPPC, which store the current line number and statement number respectively. NEWPPC and NSPPC (not a charity) are normally used to store the line number and statement number to be jumped to when GOTO and GOSUB are being used.

One can use these variables to produce a sort of 'supercharged GOTO' in that you can force the computer to jump to any statement in any line.

NEWPPC is in locations 23618 and 23619, and NSPPC is in location 23620. Hence to force a jump within the program to (say) the 4th statement in line 10, use the line:

POKE 23618, 10: POKE 23619, 0: POKE 23620, 4.

Note that the POKE 23620, ... must always follow the other 2 POKES.

Generally, to force a jump to the nth statement in line L, use the line:

POKE 23618, L −256 * INT (L/256): POKE 23619,
                        INT (L/256): POKE 23620,n.

The second POKE may be omitted if L is less than 256. If you ever find yourself in a situation where you want to insert an extra line into a block of program, there is not a spare line number and no 'renumber' facility is available, then you could insert the extra line as an extra statement in the line above it and use the above technique to 'GOTO' the statement as required. This is however a cumbersome process and any possible use of a GOSUB to a subroutine in a 'less cluttered' part of the program is to be much preferred.

CHAPTER 13
CHANGING MODES

MODE

This system variable occupies location 23617 and despite the
manual, the programmer can only use it to force a graphic (G)
mode prompt or an extended (E) mode prompt in the next INPUT
statement.

In graphics mode, MODE has the value 2 (bit 1 is set). In
extended mode, MODE has the value 1 (bit 0 is set, only valid
for one keystroke, as usual). Hence to force a graphic—mode
INPUT for A$, use:

                POKE 23617, 2: INPUT A$

For extended mode use:

                POKE 23617, 1: INPUT A$.

Unless A$ in the latter example becomes the empty string, the
E—mode will return to L—mode after the first keystroke. If
however A$ is empty or G—mode has been 'forced', then the mode
will remain the same for the next INPUT statement. Hence to
restore the prompt to the normal 'L', we use:

                POKE 23617, 0

POKEing extended mode before an INPUT can be particularly
useful if repeated BIN functions are being entered.

CAPS LOCK

Having just mentioned how to produce G- and E-mode INPUTS, I will 'jump the gun' up to location 23658, which is one of those mysterious system variables given the description "more flags" in the Spectrum Manual.

When the CAPS LOCK is on, bit 3 (value 8) of this location is set. When the CAPS LOCK is taken off, the bit is reset (value 0). Hence to change all INPUTs and INKEY$ to capitals in a program, use:

POKE 23658, 8;

and to produce 'lower case' or 'small letter' INPUTs and INKEY$,

POKE 23658, 0.

This technique is a valuable alternative solution to the problem discussed on page 72 regarding the fact that INKEY$ = "Y" is different to INKEY$ = "y".

Hence instead of using the 'clumsy' lines such as:

```
120 IF INKEY$ = 'Y' OR INKEY$ = 'y' THEN PRINT
    "YES"
130 IF INKEY$ = 'N' OR INKEY$ = 'm' THEN PRINT
    "NO"
```

we can use:

```
120 POKE 23658, 8 : IF INKEY$ = 'Y' THEN PRINT
    "YES"
130 IF INKEY$ = 'N' THEN PRINT "NO"
```

The use of this concept is most efficient when dealing with a large number of conditional INPUT or INKEY$ statements.

CHAPTER 14
SCREEN COLOURS

BORDCR

Although the Spectrum normally protects the user from
accidentally setting the INK and PAPER for the two INPUT lines
at the bottom of the screen to the same colour, you can if you
wish, do so by POKEing the system variable BORDCR, location
23624. This may prove particularly useful if your computer is
on show and you wish to discourage prying little fingers from
ruining your program listing.

To produce the required effect:

                POKE 23624, 8 * BORDERCOLOUR + INKCOLOUR : CLS
                              (the PAPER)

The CLS can be omitted if the computer is in 'direct command'
mode. The above line will change the INK and PAPER of the
bottom 2 lines of the screen, but to produce the appropriate
BORDER colour at the same time the line should be preceeded by
a BORDER command.

It is interesting to note that by using the above POKE location
we can make the input lines FLASH and/or BRIGHTer by adding the
following values to the number to be POKEd in:

                128 for FLASH 1
                64 for BRIGHT 1

The new value of BORDCR remains unaffected until the next
BORDER or NEW command.

EXAMPLE

(This one is particularly sickly!) To produce a magenta border
with yellow INK and magenta PAPER INPUT lines, FLASH 1 and
BRIGHT 1, use the line

          BORDER 3: POKE 23624, 128 + 64 + 3 * 8 + 6: CLS

ATTR P, MASK P, ATTR T, MASK T

These variables simply store the values of INK, PAPER, BRIGHT
and FLASH that are currently being used. The 'P' stands for
Permanent and the 'T' for Temporary (i.e. enclosed in and only
operative on the current PRINT statement).

ATTR P and ATTR T are of little use; but for reference here are
the values which are added to make them:

          ATTR = 8 * (PAPER COLOUR) + INK Colour + (128 for
FLASH 1) + (64 for BRIGHT 1)

ATTR P is in location 23693 and ATTR T is at address 23695.

MASK P and MASK T are more useful; any 'bit' of the one-byte
variables that is a 1 shows that the corresponding attribute
bit for PRINTing is to be taken from the cell at the current
PRINT position on the screen (as in the case of INK, PAPER,
BRIGHT and FLASH 8).

MASK P is at location 23694 and MASK T is at 23696. the main
point of interest with these variables is that we can set not
only the INK and PAPER to 8 but we can also restrict the effect
to only 1 or 2 of the 3 primary (blue, red and green) colours
that make up the eight available colours. This principle is
explained more fully with the SCREENOP routines in Chapter 3.
The constituent values for MASK P and MASK T are as follows:

BIT	EFFECT	VALUE
0	BLUE INK 8	1
1	RED INK 8	2
2	GREEN INK 8	4
3	BLUE PAPER 8	8
4	RED PAPER 8	16
5	GREEN PAPER 8	32
6	BRIGHT 8	64
7	FLASH 8	128

		255

CHAPTER 15
FRAMES:- THE HIDDEN TIMER

Hidden away in the darkest recesses of the system variables is
a constantly changing counter called FRAMES. This counter is
incremented 50 times per second in the U.K. and 60 times per
second in N. America. This frequency is equal to the mains
frequency in the area, and also to the number of times per
second a new 'frame' is sent to the television to update the
picture.

FRAMES starts off at zero when the computer is switched on and
increments every 20 milliseconds (16 2/3 in N. America) unless
a BEEP command, a cassette tape operation or one of the
hardware add-ons to the Spectrum (e.g. printer) is being used.
From this information we can at last see justification for the
1/50 or 1/60 of a second being the limit of a PAUSE statement.
"PAUSE n" simply means "wait until FRAMES has increased by n".

FRAMES is located in 3 bytes: 23672, 23673, 23674. Each byte
has eight bits and so the maximum value of FRAMES is $2^{24} - 1 =$
16777215, which in the U.K. corresponds to a time of 3 days, 21
hours, 12 minutes and 24.3 seconds since the count was started.
Hence if you leave your computer on for slightly longer than
this then FRAMES will go back to zero and start counting again.

The value of FRAMES can be found with the line:

        PRINT PEEK 23672 + 256 * PEEK 23673 + 65536 *
PEEK 23674

This program demonstrates:

```
10 REM *** To watch FRAMES ***
20 LET FRAMES=23672
30 POKE FRAMES,O: POKE FRAMES+
1,0: POKE FRAMES+2,O
40 PRINT AT 11,11;"FRAMES=";
50 PRINT AT 11,18;PEEK FRAMES+
256*PEEK (FRAMES+1)+65536*PEEK (
FRAMES+2)
60 GO TO 50
```

The hidden potential of FRAMES is vast; it can be used to drive
a clock, to monitor a time limit in a game, to power an 'alarm
clock' (a good example of which can be found in "Over the
Spectrum", another Melbourne House book) or to run a stopwatch,
as in the following program. This program gives you all the
features to be found on a normal electronic stopwatch, with a
reading in tenths of a second. Since FRAMES is accurate to
0.01% (i.e. about 9 seconds a day), so is this stopwatch. More
information on FRAMES can be found in Chapter 18, page 129 of
the Spectrum Manual.

This listing is for areas with mains frequency 50 Hz; so if you
live in N. America (60 Hz), change these values in line 150:

1.8 E5	to	2.16 E5
3 E3	to	3.6 E3
50	to	60
5	to	6

And in line 130:

4320 000 to 5184 000

```
10 REM ** STOPWATCH *** © Davi
d M. Webb 1982
20 PAPER 5: BORDER 5: INK 0: C
LS
30 REM
40 REM T=TIME
50 REM
60 PRINT AT 9,13; INK 2; PAPER
6;"STOPWATCH"
70 PRINT AT 0,0;"PRESS:": PRIN
T  BRIGHT 1;"L"; BRIGHT 0;" for
Lap time": PRINT  BRIGHT 1;"R";
BRIGHT 0;" to return to stopwatc
h": PRINT  BRIGHT 1;"S"; BRIGHT
0;" to Start": PRINT  BRIGHT 1;"
SPACE"; BRIGHT 0;" to stop, THEN
 ": PRINT  BRIGHT 1;"C"; BRIGHT
0;" to continue": PRINT  BRIGHT
1;"X"; BRIGHT 0;" to reset stopw
atch"
80 POKE 23658,8: REM caps lock
```

```
  90 PLOT 100,89: DRAW 86,0: DRA
W 0,-12: DRAW -86,0: DRAW 0,12:
REM display window
 100 PRINT AT 11,13;"0 :0 :0.0 "
 110 PAUSE 0: IF INKEY$<>"S" THE
N  GO TO 100: REM START
 120 POKE 23672,0: POKE 23673,0:
 POKE 23674,0
 130 LET T=PEEK 23672+256*PEEK 2
3673+65536*PEEK 23674: IF T>4320
000 THEN  GO TO 120: REM ARE 24
HOURS UP?
 140 LET T1=T
 150 PRINT AT 11,13;INT (T/1.8E5
);TAB 15;":";: LET T=T-1.8E5*INT
 (T/1.8E5): PRINT INT (T/3E3);TA
B 18;":";
 155 LET T=T-3E3*INT (T/3E3): PR
INT INT (T/50);".";: LET T=T-50*
INT (T/50): PRINT INT (T/50);TAB
 23: IF INKEY$="L" THEN  PAUSE 0
 160 IF INKEY$<>" " THEN  GO TO
130
 170 LET F3=INT (T1/65536): LET
T1=T1-65536*F3: LET F2=INT (T1/2
56): LET F1=T1-256*F2: REM F1,F2
,F3 ARE FRAME VALUES WHEN WATCH
WAS STOPPED
 180 PAUSE 0: IF INKEY$="C" THEN
 POKE 23672,F1: POKE 23673,F2:
POKE 23674,F3: GO TO 130
 190 IF INKEY$="X" THEN  GO TO 1
00: REM RESET STOPWATCH
 200 GO TO 180
```

PRESS:
L for Lap time
R to return to stopwatch
S to Start
SPACE to stop, THEN
C to continue
X to reset stopwatch

STOPWATCH

```
| 0 :1 :9.0 |
```

CHAPTER 16
SCROLLING THE SCREEN

One problem frequently encountered by BASIC programmers on the Spectrum is how to stop the "scroll?" prompt appearing and how to make the screen scroll at will, as the useful SCROLL command on the ZX-81 has for some reason been omitted from Spectrum BASIC.

There is a system variable called SCR CT (for SCRoll CounT), and this has a value of one more than the number of lines the screen will be scrolled upwards by before stopping with "scroll?" (hence normally SCR CT is less than or equal to 23). Therefore, to keep the computer from stopping, we must POKE a value of SCR CT greater than one (255 will do).

SCR CT can be found at location 23692. This little program shows you how it works:

```
10 PRINT AT 21, 31'
20 PRINT PEEK 23692
30 GOTO 20
```

Line 10 forces the first "scroll?" prompt. Note that the PEEK function in line 20 is evaluated before PRINTing starts, hence the value printed corresponds to the state of SCR CT after the previous number had been PRINTed.

To stop "scroll?" occuring use:

```
POKE 23692, 255
```

and preferably do this in a program loop so that the value of SCR CT never reaches 1, as it otherwise would after the screen had scrolled 254 times.

To simulate a ZX-81-type SCROLL, do this:

POKE 23692, 255: PRINT AT 21, 31 ' ' AT 21, 0;

(Note the two single apostrophes). This makes the computer prepare for printing on the next (as yet unseen) line below the bottom line of the user's screen area, and in doing so SCROLLS the screen up a line and sets the 'print position' at 21,0. Allow me to elucidate:

```
  10 LET a$="Press any key to SC
ROLL me."
  20 PRINT a$
  30 PAUSE 0: REM WAIT
  40 POKE 23692,255: PRINT AT 21
,31''AT 21,0;: REM SCROLL
  50 PRINT a$: REM PRINT POSITIO
N HAS BEEN SET TO 21,0
  60 GO TO 30
```

There is, in fact, another way of producing a SCROLL-type function. In the Spectrum ROM at address 3582 begins the routine that performs the actual scroll that we can force, as shown above, from BASIC. This machine-code routine can be called using the USR function, like so:

RANDOMIZE USR 3582.

This will scroll the screen up a line. Note that the PRINT position is unaltered, and so to imitate the ZX-81 SCROLL we must use:

RANDOMIZE USR 3582: PRINT AT 21, 0;

Incidently and conversely, if you wish to produce a "scroll?" prompt then:

POKE 23692, 1: PRINT AT 21, 31''

or the 'direct call' version,

RANDOMIZE USR 3213

will do nicely!

CHAPTER 17
REDEFINING THE CHARACTER SET: 96 MORE GRAPHICS

Apart from the fact that twenty-one user-definable graphic
characters are available on the Spectrum, it is also possible
to redefine the 96 characters (CODES 32 to 127, SPACE to (c))
whose normal "patterns" are held in a table in the ROM.

The character table begins at address 15616 and ends at address
16383 (the last byte of the ROM). Just like user defined
graphic characters, the entry for each character in the table
consists of eight consecutive bytes, one for each 'row' of the
character. Each byte has, of course, eight bits, one for each
column. The entries in the table are arranged in order of
character CODE. Let me demonstrate with a program that examines
the table and reproduces the characters at 16 times normal
size:

```
   10 REM Letter, © David M. Webb
   20 PAPER 2: INK 7: BORDER 2: C
LS
   30 FOR A=15616 TO 15616+95*8 S
TEP 8: REM 96 CHARACTERS
   40 FOR B=A TO A+7: REM CHARACT
ERS HAS EIGHT ROWS
   50 LET B$="": LET C=PEEK B
   60 FOR D=0 TO 7: REM EACH ROW
HAS EIGHT BITS (1..0)
   70 LET B$=B$+("  " AND C*2<256
)+("  " AND C*2>=256): REM IS TH
E BIT AN INK(1) OR A PAPER(0) DO
T
```

```
 80 LET C=C*2-256*(C>127)
 90 NEXT D
100 PRINT B$'B$
110 NEXT B
120 BEEP .2,30
130 PRINT AT 0,0
140 NEXT A
```

Some copies of the screen:

There is a two-byte system variable called CHARS, the value of
which is 256 less than the address of the character table (i.e.
usually equal to 15360). CHARS can be found in locations 23606
and 23607, and hence its value can be checked by:

PRINT "CHARS = "; PEEK 23606 + 256 * PEEK 23607.

The great virtue of CHARS being a system variable is that we
can move the 'base address' of the table to wherever we like by
altering CHARS, and then if the new base address is in an
appropriate area of spare RAM we can redefine part or all of
the characters, just as we can with user-defined graphics.

This gimmicky little program "encodes" any phrase you INPUT by
moving the base of the table up by one character (eight bytes)
so that 'A' becomes 'B', 'C' becomes 'D' and so on. The string
is printed out with the new character set and then CHARS is
POKEd back to normal.

```
10 INPUT A$
20 PRINT "In code that is";
30 POKE 23606, 8
40 PRINT A$
50 POKE 23606, 0
```

It is very important to note that, although the 'pattern'
representing each CODE is different if CHARS is altered, the
actual meanings of all the command- and function-words are
exactly the same; the computer simply represents these words
with numbers or "tokens", so that while

PRINT A$ would look like QSJOU!B%

in the above program LISTing, it would still mean "print out A$
on the screen" to the computer. In other words, altering the
character table does not affect normal usage of the machine –
it just makes listings and text nearly impossible for the user
to understand! To see what I mean, leave out line 50 of the
above program and press (ENTER) after it has RUN.

Right then, enough of that gimmickry and on to more serious
applications of CHARS. You may well find a time when you have
used up all the 21 user-defined graphics available on the
Spectrum, or when you want the BASIC SCREEN$ to recognise your
graphic characters. This is the time to call on a technique for
changing the character table.

First of all, we need to CLEAR an area of memory to accommodate
the new table. Using all the characters, this will be 96 x 8 =
768 bytes long. Next it is usually a good idea to copy the
existing table into the new table area. We then alter CHARS
appropriately so that it is 256 less than the address of the
start of the new table. At this stage things will appear as
normal, since the new table is exactly the same as the old one.
It is, however, in RAM. We can therefore redefine any character
we like using the BIN function in a very similar way to that
used with the user-defined graphic characters (see Chapter 14,
page 92 of the Spectrum manual).

If at any time you wish to revert to the normal table,

POKE 23606, 0: POKE 23607, 60.

I have written the following program partly for its functional
usefulness and partly to illustrate how to manipulate the
character set using the procedure outlined above. With the
program, you will be able to move, alter, SAVE and reLOAD any
character set you desire. To exercise the SAVE option, enter as
a direct command

GOTO 300

All other options are presented automatically when the program
is RUN. Please feel free to make alterations and improvements
to the program – you could for example add the option of
defining the characters by moving a cursor over an 8 by 8 grid.
It is obvious that having so many more graphics characters
available dramatically improves the quality of many games: I
leave it to the reader to further exploit CHARS.

```
  10 REM To redefine the cha
racter set
  20 REM first we clear some spa
ce
  30 GO SUB 310
  40 INPUT "Shall I clear some m
ore space?";A$: IF A$<>"Y" AND A
$<>"y" THEN  GO TO 60
```

```
 50 CLEAR RAMTOP-768: REM 768=8
*(NUMBER OF CHARACTERS ROUTINES)
 60 GO SUB 310
 70 REM NOW WE COPY UP THE OLD
TABLE
 80 INPUT "Shall I copy up the
old table ?";A$: IF A$<>"Y" AND
A$<>"y" THEN  GO TO 110
 90 INPUT "Shall I LOAD a table
 from tape?";A$: IF A$="Y" OR A$
="y" THEN  LOAD ""CODE RAMTOP+1,
768
 100 GO TO 150
 110 PRINT "Hang on...": FOR a=1
 TO 768
 120 POKE RAMTOP+a,PEEK (15615+a
)
 130 NEXT a
 140 REM THEN WE ALTER CHARS
 150 LET CHARS=RAMTOP+1-256
 160 POKE 23606,CHARS-256*INT (C
HARS/256)
 170 POKE 23607,INT (CHARS/256)
 180 PRINT "The value of CHARS i
s ";CHARS
 190 REM FINALLY WE DEFINE ANY C
HARACTERS
 200 GO SUB 310: INPUT "Alter wh
ich character?"; LINE A$
 205 PRINT CODE A$;A$
 210 IF LEN A$<>1 OR CODE A$<32
OR CODE A$>127 THEN  GO TO 200
 220 LET ENTRY=RAMTOP+1+8*(CODE
A$-32): REM THAT IS WHERE THE PA
TTERN IS
 230 FOR R=0 TO 7: REM ONE ROW A
T A TIME USE THE BIN FUNCTION TO
 INPUT THE PATTERN
 235 POKE 23617,1: REM EXTENDED
MODE
 240 INPUT ("ROW ";R;" ";);ROW:
IF ROW<0 OR ROW>255 THEN  GO TO
240
 250 POKE ENTRY+R,ROW
 260 NEXT R
 270 GO TO 200
 280 REM SPECIAL SAVE SECTION
 290 GO SUB 310
 300 SAVE "Characters"CODE RAMTO
P+1,768: STOP
 310 LET RAMTOP=PEEK 23730+256*P
EEK 23731
 320 RETURN
 330 REM © DAVID M. WEBB 1983
```

CHAPTER 18
MEMORY LABELS

There is a whole group of system variables or 'labels' which
the computer uses to 'keep an eye' on the state of its memory
for example to know where the program begins, where the BASIC
variables start and so on. Most of these labels are of little
interest to the programmer: detailed here are the ones that are
worth noting.

1. PROG

Locations 23635 and 23636 tell the computer where the PROGram
starts.

         PRINT PEEK 23635 + 256 * PEEK 23636

gives the value of PROG. Add five to this and you have the
location of the first character after the REM statement, if the
first program line is

            10 REM Lots of characters to store machine code
in.

Hence if you wish to store machine code in a REM statement at
the beginning of the program, then you simply create a long
enough REM statement (one character per byte) and find the
start address by adding five to the value of PROG. Note that
without any microdrives etc. attached, PROG is always equal to
23755.

The other possible use of PROG is to produce a more permanent

copyright statement at the beginning of the program. First
enter the copyright line in the usual way at the beginning of
the program, then evaluate PROG and finally

POKE (PROG), O: POKE (PROG + 1), O

If the old line number is less than 256 then the first of the 2
commands can be omitted. What the procedure does is to
'renumber' the first line of the program to zero, thereby
making it impossible to EDIT or remove the line without POKEing
the number back above zero again. A zero first line number can
also be produced with the machine code renumber routine in this
book, as explained in Chapter 24.

2. VARS

VARS holds the address of the BASIC VARiables, and is itself
held in locations 23627 and 23628, so its value can be found by

PRINT PEEK 23627 + 256 * PEEK 23628

The BASIC variables are situated directly after the BASIC
program in the Spectrum memory, and hence we can find the
actual length of a program by subtracting PROG from VARS, thus:

PRINT "Program is"; 256 * (PEEK 23628 − PEEK
23636)
+ PEEK 23627 − PEEK 23635; "bytes long".

− quite a mouthful but the only way in BASIC (see Chapter 23
for the equivalent machine code routine).

3. RAMTOP and STKEND

I have put these two otherwise unrelated system variables
together because they can be used to estimate the amount of
memory left to the user. Refering to page 165 of the Spectrum
Manual you will notice that the only things between the
pointers STKEND and RAMTOP on the memory map are spare memory
and the usually small machine stack and GOSUB stack.

RAMTOP is evaluated by:

PRINT PEEK 23730 + 256 * PEEK 23731

and STKEND by:

PRINT PEEK 23653 + 256 * PEEK 23654

Alternatively, as luck would have it, the Spectrum ROM contains
a routine that returns the value of STKEND, thus:

PRINT USR 7962

To estimate the amount of memory left then, just subtract
STKEND from RAMTOP. All this can obviously be a tedious
process, so if you intend to use the function frequently it is

probably as well to use the more accurate (it doesn't count the 2 stacks) machine code routine in Chapter 23.

4. DATADD

If you have 'READ' an unknown way along a DATA line and suddenly have to do a CLEAR or a RESTORE command to another line then you will lose your position on the first DATA line. Should you wish to retain it, DATADD may be of use.

DATADD holds the address of the comma after the last DATA item that was READ in the program, and can be found at address 23639, so to store the position on the line,

              LET DATADD = PEEK 23639 + 256 * PEEK 23640

Then whenever (if ever) you wish to go back to that position after DATADD has been altered, you can restore DATADD (excuse my pun) as follows:

                   POKE 23640, INT (DATADD/256)
                   POKE 23639, DATADD - 256 * INT (DATADD/256)

5. UDG

UDG holds the address of the first user-defined graphic character (CHR$ 144) and is itself held in locations 23675 and 23676. There are 21 user-defined characters, and hence the length of memory they ocupy is 21 x 8 bytes = 168 bytes. Conveniently enough, this is less than the 256 bytes to be found in the area normally used by the printer, the PRINTER BUFFER.

If you are:
a)   running out of memory, and
b)   not using the ZX printer,

then you can increase the spare memory left for your program by 168 bytes by moving the user defined graphics from the top of memory down to the printer buffer and then CLEARing RAMTOP to the last byte of free memory.

The printer buffer is 256 bytes long and begins at address 23296. Many of the routines in this book use the early part of the buffer as a storage area, so to 'play safe' we will take the last 168 bytes of the buffer in this case.

This program moves the graphics and alters UDG.

Note that, as always, UDG = USR "a"

```
                   10 REM 'GRAPHIC SHIFT'
                   20 LET NEWUDG = 23384
                   30 FOR A = 0 TO 167
                   40 POKE NEWUDG + A, PEEK (USR "a" + A)
                   50 NEXT A
```

```
60 REM ADJUST UDG
70 POKE 23676, INT (NEWUDG/256)
80 POKE 23675, NEWUDG - 256 * INT (NEWUDG/256)
```

Precisely the same function is fulfilled by a fast, short
machine language routine:

```
HEX.        ;MEMORY LABELS  LENGTH: 16 BYTES
            UDG    EQU   5C7BH
2A7B5C      START  LD    HL,(UDG)     ;HL=OLD UDG.
ED5B585B           LD    DE,(5B58H)   ;DE=NEW UDG.
ED537B5C           LD    (UDG),DE     ;STORE NEW UDG.
01A800             LD    BC,168       ;BLOCK SHIFT 168 BYTES
EDB0               LDIR               ;OF GRAPHICS.
C9                 RET                ;RETURN TO BASIC.
                   END
```

We have not quite finished; to create new spare memory we must
increase RAMTOP by 168 to its maximum value of 32767 (16K
machines) or 65535 (48K). Simply do this with a CLEAR command:
        CLEAR 32767 (16K) or CLEAR 65535 (48K)

It is perhaps worth mentioning that another way of doing a
'block shift' of the graphics (or any other data for that
matter) is to SAVE it from one address using SAVE... CODE m,n
and then LOAD back to another address using LOAD... CODE. This
can be, and in most cases is, the slowest and clumsiest method
for block shifting, but if you have a Microdrive then it may
well prove to be highly practicable.

CHAPTER 19
DF SZ AND SOFTWARE PROTECTION.

DFSZ holds the number of lines in the lower INPUT part of the screen. This is normally two, but can be altered with care.

On the earlier ZX-81 machine it was quite feasible to PRINT on the two INPUT lines by POKEing DF SZ to zero and then using "PRINT AT 22,0..." or "PRINT AT 23,0...". In the case of the Spectrum, one must be more careful when DFSZ is set to zero, if one is to avoid a "crash".

Since DFSZ holds the number of lines in the INPUT and message area of the screen, if it is reduced right down to zero then there is no room for messages or "reports" to be printed, and whenever the computer tries to print in this area, due to the lack of a "failsafe" device in the ROM which would alter DFSZ to make room for the message, the computer crashes. So, if you must alter DFSZ to zero, then remember the following points:

1. Do not use any INPUTS or SAVE commands.

2. Do not allow the Spectrum to try and print "Scroll?".

3. Do not press "BREAK" or the Spectrum will try to print a report and line number, etc.

4. Do not use "PRINT AT 23,..." This is because for some reason the ROM has been programmed only to accept rows 0 to 22, and so "PRINT AT 23,..." would produce an attempt to print the error report "B Integer out of range".

DFSZ can be altered to between 1 and 24 with none of the above problems and if altered to 1 then "PRINT AT 22,..." is acceptable. In order to reach the very bottom line if DFSZ is zero, (PRINT AT 22, 31 ') will have to be used, since "PRINT AT 23,..." is unacceptable.

There is, as luck would have it, a far better solution to the problem hidden away in Sinclair BASIC. It would seem that whoever wrote the Spectrum manual either forgot to mention or didn't want us to know that there exists a function allowing you to print in the input area. I stumbled on it one day during one of those "I-can't-think-what-to-write" sessions.

To print in the area (using the "AT" coordinates found in some INPUT statements) use:

PRINT # 0 ; (normal print items)

In fact there are 4 values that currently follow "#" (the Microdrives may use more), they are 0 and 1 for printing in the lower half of the screen, 2 for printing in the upper part (as normal) and 3 for sending items to the printer (as in LPRINT).

PROTECTING BASIC PROGRAMS

Point 3. above can come in handy if you want to stop people "breaking into" and copying your BASIC programs. By POKEing DFSZ to zero you ensure that any attempt to BREAK the program will produce a distinctly unconscious Spectrum. This idea would be best used in conjunction with the following SAVEing technique.

As you probably know, you can stop a program "auto-running" from tape when it has been stored with a SAVE... LINE... command by first NEWing the computer and then using MERGE " " rather than LOAD " ". This has proven to be rather a problem for software companies who were trying to prevent copying of their programs. One way round the problem is to SAVE the program as a block of code by inserting the following lines at the end of a program:

```
9010 LET STKEND = PEEK 23653 + 256 * PEEK 23654
9020 SAVE " [name] " CODE 23552, STKEND -23500
9030 RUN
```

This SAVEs the entire user area, including program, calculator stack, BASIC variables and system variables as a block of code onto tape, so that when the whole lot is brought back using a LOAD "(name)" CODE command the computer carries on exactly where it left off, i.e. by executing line 9030, RUN.

Now obviously you cannot MERGE a block of code, but it is not impossible for someone to CLEAR RAMTOP to a low enough address, LOAD the code up immediately above it, decipher the old value of STKEND in order to calculate the length of the block and then to re-SAVE it onto a new tape. In order to counter this possibility you could substitute the following lines:

```
9010 LET STKEND = PEEK 23653 + 256 * PEEK 23654
9020 LET A = INT(RND * 256)
9030 SAVE " [name] " CODE 23552 - A, STKEND -
      23500 + A
9040 RUN
```

This introduces a new element of randomness in that our phantom
copier does not now know from which address the code is SAVEd,
since a part of the printer buffer of random length A is also
SAVEd at the beginning of the block of code, thereby dislodging
STKEND to an unknown position in the block. Hopefully at this
point our "pirate" will have given up and moved on to someone
else's less-protected program, but it has to be said that
ultimately it is possible to break into any program given time
and patience - we can only make it harder to do so.

CHAPTER 20
MISCELLANEOUS SYSTEM VARIABLES

1. S TOP

S TOP, for Screen TOP, holds the number of the program line
which appears at the top of the screen in automatic listings.
STOP can be found in locations 23660 and 23661.

2. OLDPPC and OSPCC

OLDPPC and OSPCC hold the line number and statement number
respectively that CONTINUE would jump to after a "BREAK into
program". Hence if you have just stopped the program, pressed
newline which deletes the message, and can't remember what line
you were at, then these variables will tell you.

        PRINT PEEK 23662 + 256 * PEEK 23663

will tell you which line number is next, and

        PRINT PEEK 23664

will tell you which statement.

3. COORDS

Addresses 23677 and 23678 respectively hold the X and Y
coordinates of the last point plotted. These can be treated as
two extra BASIC variables when using a PLOTing or DRAWing
program; if you start a program with

```
LET XO = 23677: LET YO = 23678
```

then whenever you need to know the last point plotted,

```
PEEK XO and PEEK YO will be fine.
```

To draw a line from the last point plotted to (A, B)

```
DRAW A - PEEK XO, B - PEEK YO
```

You can also POKE COORDS to alter the PLOT position without actually PLOTting a point or DRAWing a line.

S POSN

S POSN holds the current print position, but not in the way that you would expect. If you have just PRINTed at A, B then

```
location 23688 holds 33 - B,
location 23689 holds 24 - A.
```

Hence to find your current print position in the "conventional" format (A, B):

```
LET A = 24 - PEEK 23689
LET B = 33 - PEEK 23688
```

If you intend to use this a lot in any one program (perhaps in conjunction with SCREEN$), then it is worth using DEF FN statements for the two values, i.e.

```
:DEF FN Y() = 24 - PEEK 23689
:DEF FN X() = 33 - PEEK 23688
```

SEED

Seed is the system variable that was used to generate the last 'random' number, and is located at addresses 23670 and 23671. Try this:

```
PRINT RND, (PEEK 23670 + 256 * PEEK
23671)/65536.
```

You will see that the two values printed are equal. Every time RND is used, SEED is altered by the computer as follows:

```
New SEED = (75 (SEED + 1)) mod 65537 -1
```

This corresponds to the BASIC line

```
LET SEED = 75 * (SEED + 1): LET SEED = SEED
-65537 * INT (SEED/65537) -1
```

The new value of SEED is stored away and then divided by 65536 to produce a value of RND between 0 and 1, the latter being exclusive.

Whenever RANDOMIZE is used, this just moves the first two bytes
of FRAMES into SEED, so that the next time RND is used the
computer will produce a psuedo-random number at a different
position in the sequence of 65536 different numbers that the
above function generates.

This shows that FRAMES is moved into SEED by RANDOMIZE.

```
10 RANDOMIZE
20 LET SEED - PEEK 23670 + 256 * PEEK 23671
30 LET FRAMES = PEEK 23672 + 256 * PEEK 23673
40 PRINT "SEED ="; SEED, "FRAMES ="; FRAMES
```

There will be a small difference between SEED and FRAMES since
FRAMES is still increasing while the program is being RUN.

DFCC and DFCCL

These two variables hold the address in the display file of the
two print positions, one for the top part of the screen and the
other for the INPUT area. Due to the odd arrangement of the
display file it is not normally desirable to PEEK and POKE the
screen; we have POINT, PRINT and SCREEN$ (see SCREEN$2, an
improved function in this book) for that. The actual layout of
the memory map is explained fully on page 164 of the Spectrum
Manual, and as a consequence of this layout, if the print
position is Y, X then

$$DFCC = 2048 * INT (Y/8 + 8) + (Y - 8 * INT (Y/8)) * 32 + X.$$

Don't forget that each character on the screen is stored in
eight bytes in memory (one for each row). The addresses of the
eight bytes for any one character are 256 apart, and so if the
first row is at DFCC, then the second is at DFCC + 256, the
third at DFCC + 512 and so on. This program will illustrate; a
graphic character is POKEd into a random position and then
animated by further POKEing. Line 20 sets the print position
and then line 30 reads DFCC, which is located at addresses
23684 and 23685. As you will see, the effect produced by
POKEing instead of PRINTing is considerably slower than the
latter and I can think of no reason to justify its substitution
for the same in normal BASIC programming.

```
  10 REM POKING TO PRINT
  15 BORDER 0: PAPER 0: INK 6: C
LS
  20 PRINT AT INT (RND*22),INT (
RND*32);
  30 LET DFCC=PEEK 23684+256*PEE
K 23685
  40 FOR C=0 TO 1
  50 FOR A=DFCC TO DFCC+7*256 ST
EP 256
  60 READ B: POKE A,B: NEXT A
  70 NEXT C
```

```
   80 RESTORE : GO TO 40
   90 DATA 24,60,126,25,31,254,60
,24
  100 DATA 248,60,23,15,15,23,60,
248
```

PFLAG

This system variable holds the "switches" or FLAGS for the
printing values PAPER 9, INK 9, INVERSE and OVER. There are two
bits for each of these; one for the temporary value and one for
the permanent one. The temporary values are those caused by
inserting the functions into a PRINT statement in order to
affect just that command, the permanent ones are used
otherwise. Here are the values:

FUNCTION	TEMPORARY		PERMANENT	
	BIT	VALUE	BIT	VALUE
OVER 1	0	1	1	2
INVERSE 1	2	4	3	8
INK 9	4	16	5	32
PAPER 9	6	64	7	128

P FLAG is situated in location 23697, and by adding up the
values of the functions desired from the table above, you can
set them all in one go by POKEing P FLAG.

Hence to set a permanent OVER 1; INVERSE 1; INK 9; PAPER 9;
just

                POKE 23697, 170

- a lot more succinct, and memory-saving!

ROUTINES TO IMPROVE BASIC COMMANDS

CHAPTER 21
SCREEN$ 2

If you have ever tried to use the SCREEN$ function on the
Spectrum to recognise a user-defined graphic character (such as
a space invader) or one of those "chunky" graphic characters
that consists of four squares or "blocks", each of which may be
INK or PAPER, then you will have found that the function does
not work and that the result is an empty string. This can be
illustrated with a short program:

```
10 PRINT AT 10, 15; " ▞ "
20 PRINT AT 1, 1; "The character at (10, 15) is
   "; SCREEN$ (0,0)
```

In this case the character that the function does not recognise
is CHR$ (137), but the same applies to all characters whose
CODE ranges from 129 to 164 (if the CODE is greater than 164,
then the corresponding "keyword" is made up of characters
recognised by SCREEN$).

This deficiency in SCREEN$ makes it almost useless, since it is
usually needed when writing graphical games (e.g. to detect
whether you, the defender are about to be annihilated by an
alien's carelessly placed mask grenade). For this reason I
bring to you an alternative SCREEN$, named SCREEN$2 (points for
imagination...?).

SCREEN$2 will look at any character 'cell' on the screen and
come back to you with its CODE. If there is no character, but
just a selection of PLOTted points on that cell, then the
result will be zero.

HOW TO USE SCREEN$2

Take the coordinates of the cell (these range from (0, 0) to
(23, 31) and POKE them into addresses 23354 and 23355
respectively. So for SCREEN$ (10, 21):

                    POKE 23354, 10
                    POKE 23355, 21

Now, if you intend to "call" the routine more than once, it is
easiest to define a variable:

            LET SCREEN = (start address of SCREEN$)

Thirdly and finally, you use the USR function to return the
character at cell (L, C) (for Lines, Columns). This is best
illustrated by showing a sample of program lines using SCREEN$
(most of which may not work) and their equivalents using the
machine code routine (all of which will).

Using SCREEN$	Using SCREEN$2
LET L = 5 : LET C = 10	POKE 23354, 5 : POKE 23355 10
	LET SCREEEN=[start address]
LET A$=SCREEN$(L,C)	LET A$=CHR$ USR SCREEN
	IF USR SCREEN = 144 THEN PRINT
IF CODE SCREEN$(L,C) = 144	
THEN PRINT	
"The character at (5, 10) is	"The character at (5, 10) is
a graphic a"	a graphic a"
PRINT AT 0,0;SCREEN$(L,C)	PRINT AT 0,0; CHR$ USR SCREEN

If there are character cells on your screen whose contents are
unrecognisable as a character, and there is a possibility that
your program will test those cells with SCREEN$2, then in that
case the value zero will be sent back after using the routine.

Now obviously

                PRINT CHR$ USR SCREEN

will not then make a great deal of sense to the Spectrum, and a
question mark will be printed. To stop this occuring, you
should incorporate the function "AND USR SCREEN" like so:

        PRINT CHR$ (USR SCREEN) AND USR SCREEN

This means

        "PRINT CHR$ (USR SCREEN) only if USR SCREEN > 0"

A longer-winded version would be:

        IF USR SCREEN <>0 THEN PRINT CHR$ USR SCREEN.

Here then is the routine, followed by a short "demo" program.

```
HEX.          ;SCREEN$2 LENGTH: 129 BYTES
              CHARS   EQU   5C36H
              UD6     EQU   5C7BH
ED4B3A5B      START   LD    BC,(5B3AH)     ;C=LINE, B=COLUMN
79                    LD    A,C            ;LOCATE THE ADDRESS OF
E618                  AND   18H            ;THE FIRST ROW OF THE
C640                  ADD   A,40H          ;CHARACTER CELL IN THE
67                    LD    H,A            ;SCREEN MEMORY.
79                    LD    A,C
87                    ADD   A,A
87                    ADD   A,A
87                    ADD   A,A
87                    ADD   A,A
87                    ADD   A,A
80                    ADD   A,B
6F                    LD    L,A            ;SET THE 'CODE' TO 32
0E20                  LD    C,20H          ;(SPACE) AND START SCANNING
ED5B365C              LD    DE,(CHARS)     ;THROUGH THE CHARACTER
14                    INC   D              ;TABLE.
E5            NXTCHAR PUSH  HL
0608                  LD    B,8            ;COMPARE EACH ROW OF THE
1A            NXTROW  LD    A,(DE)         ;CURRENT CHARACTER IN THE
BE                    CP    (HL)           ;TABLE WITH THAT OF THE
2006                  JR    NZ,HOP1        ;CHARACTER CELL, AND IF A
24                    INC   H              ;ROW IS NOT EQUAL TO THE
13                    INC   DE             ;CORRESPONDING ONE IN THE
10F8                  DJNZ  NXTROW         ;CHARACTER CELL THEN MOVE
E1                    POP   HL             ;ON TO THE NEXT CHARACTER
                                           ;IN THE TABLE.
C9                    RET                  ;IF THE CHARACTER CODE
E1            HOP1    POP   HL             ;HAS BEEN FOUND THEN RETURN
13            NXT1    INC   DE             ;TO BASIC.
10FD                  DJNZ  NXT1
0C                    INC   C
79                    LD    A,C
FEA5                  CP    0A5H
280C                  JR    Z,BLCKCHK
FE80                  CP    80H
20E5                  JR    NZ,NXTCHAR
0E90                  LD    C,90H
ED5B7B5C              LD    DE,(UD6)       ;NOW CHECK FOR A USER -
180D                  JR    NXTCHAR        ;DEFINED GRAPHIC CHARACTER.
E5            BLCKCHK PUSH  HL             ;NOW IT'S EITHER A 'CHUNKY'
0608                  LD    B,8            ;GRAPHIC OR NOT A CHARACTER
7E            NXTROW2 LD    A,(HL)         ;IN THE CELL. SO CHECK TO
3C                    INC   A              ;SEE IF THE CELL DOESN'T
2810                  JR    Z,OK           ;CONTAIN A 'CHUNKY
3D                    DEC   A              ;GRAPHIC', AND IF SO...
2800                  JR    Z,OK
FE0F                  CP    0FH
2809                  JR    Z,OK
FEF0                  CP    0F0H
2805                  JR    Z,OK
```

105

```
010000    NOCODE  LD    BC,0        ;...THEN RETURN TO BASIC
E1                POP   HL          ;WITH CODE ZERO. THE
C9                RET               ;CHARACTER IS A 'CHUNKY'
24        OK      INC   H           ;GRAPHIC CHARACTER. THIS
10E9              DJNZ  NXTROW2      ;ALGORITHM TAKES DECIMAL
E1                POP   HL          ;128 AND ADDS ON THE VALUE
0E80              LD    C,80H        ;OF ANY OF THE FOUR BLOCKS
1601              LD    D,1          ;(1,2,4,8) THAT IS INK.
1E0F      NXTHALF LD    E,0FH        ;D HOLDS THE VALUE OF THE
E5        NXT2    PUSH  HL          ;CURRENT 'BLOCK' BEING
0604              LD    B,4          ;CHECKED. B COUNTS THE ROWS
7E        NXTROW3 LD    A,(HL)       ;- THE CHARACTER IS SCANNED
A3                AND   E           ;IN TWO HALVES:- TOP
BB                CP    E           ;AND BOTTOM.
2006              JR    NZ,HOP2
24                INC   H
10F8              DJNZ  NXTROW3
79                LD    A,C
82                ADD   A,D
4F                LD    C,A
CB22      HOP2    SLA   D           ;D IS DOUBLED.
7B                LD    A,E
87                ADD   A,A
87                ADD   A,A
87                ADD   A,A
87                ADD   A,A
5F                LD    E,A
E1                POP   HL
20E7              JR    NZ,NXT2
C862              BIT   4,D          ;IF D<>16D THEN THE
2803              JR    Z,NOTDONE    ;CALCULATION IS NOT YET
0600      DONE    LD    B,0          ;FINISHED....
C9                RET
CB04      NOTDONE SET   2,H          ;...SO MOVE ON TO THE NEXT
180A              JR    NXTHALF      ;HALF OF THE CHARACTER.
                  END
```

Here is the demonstration program: not spectacular but it gives
you a glimpse of the vastly improved potential of SCREEN$2 by
displaying all of the characters available on the Spectrum and
then using SCREEN$2 to place them elsewhere on the screen.
Notice that line 30 depends upon where you have located the
routine in memory.

```
  10 REM SCREEN$2 DEMONSTRATION
  20 FOR a=0 TO 167: POKE USR "a
"+a,INT (RND*256)
  25 NEXT a
  30 LET screen=65200
  40 POKE 23354,0: REM l
  50 POKE 23355,0: REM c
  60 FOR a=32 TO 164
  70 PRINT AT 0,0;CHR$ a
  80 PRINT AT 1,1;CHR$ (USR scre
en)  AND USR screen
  90 PAUSE 30
 100 NEXT a
```

CHAPTER 22
PAUSE MK.2

You may have noticed while programming with the PAUSE command on the ZX-Spectrum that it doesn't always work. PAUSE is supposed to wait for a given number of frames of the TV. (forever in the case of PAUSE 0) or until a key has been pressed. Unfortunately, a bug in the auto-repeat keyboard scanning routines in the original Spectrum ROM means that if you have been pressing keys just before a PAUSE line then the machine sometimes blunders blindly on into the rest of the program. This demonstration will show you what I mean; press a few keys while in the loop, stop when you hear the BEEP, and if the computer prints a message then PAUSE 0 has failed.

```
   10 FOR a=0 TO 1000
   15 REM   PRESS KEYS WHILE IN TH
IS LOOP
   20 NEXT a
   25 BEEP 1,10: REM    WHEN YOU H
EAR THIS, STOP PRESSING
   30 PAUSE 0: REM    SUPPOSED TO
WAIT FOR A KEY PRESS
   40 PRINT "I'VE FINISHED"
```

One partial solution to the problem is to substitute line 30 with

            30 IF INKEY$ = "" THEN GOTO 30

Unfortunately this is only of use when the value after the PAUSE is zero, since it does not have any timing effect in it and will thus continue until a key is pressed rather than breaking out after a fixed number of TV. frames.

Well, you've probably guessed by now that there is a quick machine code solution to the problem, and here it is. PAUSE MK.2 will allow you a bug-free PAUSE of between 0 and 255 (around five seconds). If you need a longer PAUSE then you simply call the routine several times in succession.

To use the routine, it is a good idea to define a variable

LET PAUSE = (start address)

at the beginning of the program. Then to set the duration of the pause (zero meaning, as usual, forever),

POKE PAUSE + 1, (duration (0 - 255)).

Finally to call the routine and execute the PAUSE,

RANDOMIZE USR PAUSE
or LET A = USR PAUSE.

Now for the routine.

```
HEX.          ;PAUSE MK2  LENGTH: 25 BYTES
0600    START  LD    B,0         ;B IS THE PAUSE LENGTH.
78             LD    A,B         ;IF B=0 THEN WAIT FOR
A7             AND   A           ;A KEY PRESS.
280B           JR    Z,WAIT
AF             XOR   A           ;OTHERWISE...
76      NXFRAME HALT             ;WAIT FOR AN INTERRUPT
DBFE           IN    A,(0FEH)    ;(LIKE PAUSE 1), THEN SCAN
2F             CPL               ;THE KEYBOARD.
E61F           AND   1FH
C0             RET   NZ          ;IF NO KEYS ARE PRESSED
10F7           DJNZ  NXFRAME     ;THEN WAIT FOR THE NEXT TV
C9             RET               ;FRAME, UNLESS THE PAUSE
                                 ;COUNT IS ZERO, IN WHICH
                                 ;CASE, RETURN TO BASIC.
DBFE    WAIT   IN    A,(0FEH)    ;WAIT FOR A KEY PRESS.
2F             CPL
E61F           AND   1FH
28F9           JR    Z,WAIT      ;WHEN ONE IS DETECTED,
C9             RET               ;RETURN TO BASIC.
               END
```

Going back to our short demonstration program, using PAUSE MK.2 it should now look like this:

```
    5 LET PAUSE=65000: REM START
ADDRESS
   10 FOR a=0 TO 1000
```

```
   15 REM   PRESS KEYS WHILE IN TH
IS LOOP
   20 NEXT a
   25 BEEP 1,10: REM   WHEN YOU H
EAR THIS, STOP PRESSING
   30 POKE PAUSE+1,0: RANDOMIZE U
SR PAUSE: REM WAIT FOR A KEYPRES
S
   40 PRINT "I'VE FINISHED"
```

It occurred to me while writing PAUSE MK.2 that there may be
occasions when you want to pause for an exact amount of time
without the possibility of breaking out of the pause by
accidentally touching the keyboard. Such a case could be where
a pause was required between the notes of a sonata that your
Spectrum was playing. If you used (say) PAUSE 5 then if you
pressed any keys while the music was playing the "PAUSE 5"s
would be continually broken out of and the music would speed
up. Short of timing a FOR-NEXT loop such as

                FOR A = 1 TO 10: NEXT A

there is no BASIC solution to the problem.

The following short machine code routine solves the problem
nicely and allows you to have an un-interrupted PAUSE of
between 1 and 256 (longer pauses obtainable by calling the
routine more than once). I have called the routine 'TIMELOCK',
since you can't break through it until a certain time has
elapsed.

To use the routine,

                LET TIMELOCK = (start address)
                POKE TIMELOCK + 1, (duration)

then   RANDOMIZE USR TIMELOCK
  or   LET T = USR TIMELOCK

Here comes the code!

```
   HEX.      ;TIMELOCK LENGTH: 6 BYTES
   0600      START  LD    B,0      ;B COUNTS THE PAUSE.
   76        NXT    HALT           ;WAIT FOR INTERRUPT.
   10FD             DJNZ  NXT      ;REPEAT UNTIL B=0.
   C9               RET            ;RETURN TO BASIC.
                    END
```

Note that in this routine a value of 0 POKEd into TIMELOCK + 1
corresponds to a PAUSE of 256.

UTILITY ROUTINES

CHAPTER 23
FOR YOUR INFORMATION

This section contains three short, but useful routines that
will give you information about the state of the memory in your
machine.

The first is PROGLENGTH – the length of the BASIC program in
bytes.

```
HEX.          ;PROGLENGTH LENGTH: 13 BYTES
              VARS    EQU    5C4BH
              PROG    EQU    5C53H
2A4B5C        START   LD     HL,(VARS)
ED4B535C              LD     BC,(PROG)
A7                    AND    A          ;RESET CARRY FLAG.
ED42                  SBC    HL,BC      ;VARS-PROG=PROGLENGTH
44                    LD     B,H        ;PROGLENGTH IS RETURNED IN
4D                    LD     C,L        ;THE BC REGISTER PAIR.
C9                    RET
                      END
```

To use PROGLENGTH, enter

        PRINT "Program is "; USR (start address); "
        bytes long."

The second is VARLENGTH – the number of bytes in the variables
area.

```
HEX.            ;VARLENGTH LENGTH: 13 BYTES  DATE: 1/7/83
                ELINE   EQU   5C59H
                VARS    EQU   5C4BH
2A595C          START   LD    HL,(ELINE)
ED4B4B5C                LD    BC,(VARS)
37                      SCF                  ;SET CARRY FLAG.
ED42                    SBC   HL,BC          ;ELINE-VARS-1=VARLENGTH
44                      LD    B,H            ;VARLENGTH IS RETURNED IN
4D                      LD    C,L            ;THE BC REGISTER PAIR.
C9                      RET
                        END
```

Use VARLENGTH by entering

> PRINT "Variables are "; USR (start address); " bytes long."

The final routine is FREE, which tells you the number of bytes which you are actually free to use (discounting anything above RAMTOP). It does this by subtracting the system variable STKEND from the stack pointer (SP register pair).

```
HEX.            ;FREE LENGTH: 13 BYTES
                STKEND  EQU   5C65H
210000          START   LD    HL,0
39                      ADD   HL,SP          ;TAKE STACK POINTER.
ED4B655C                LD    BC,(STKEND)
ED42                    SBC   HL,BC          ;SUBTRACT STKEND.
44                      LD    B,H            ;RETURN RESULT IN BC.
4D                      LD    C,L
C9                      RET
                        END
```

Use FREE by typing the following:

> PRINT "you have "; USR (start address); " bytes free."

You can also find the total memory used by the computer by subtracting FREE from the amount of bytes of RAM available.

Thus:

> 16K : PRINT "Bytes used: "; 16 * 1024 — USR (start address)
>
> 48K : PRINT "Bytes used: "; 48 * 1024 — USR (start address)

CHAPTER 24
RENUMBERING YOUR PROGRAMS

This routine will renumber the line numbers of your BASIC
programs, but you will have to renumber the GOSUBs, GOTOs,
LISTs, LLISTs and RUNs yourself, as the machine code routine
necessary to completely renumber a program is very long
and complex. Nonetheless, this routine has proven very useful
to me and I am sure it will be worth your while to LOAD it
into the top of memory whenever you are writing BASIC
programs. For those who are undaunted by a very long machine
code listing the full renumber appears in Chapter 28.

USING RENUMBER

You must specify two parameters; the first line number and the
"step" between line numbers (e.g. If you want the line numbers
to read 100, 110, 120... then the first line number is 100, and
the step is 10). The parameters are entered as follows:

>   POKE 23348, (First line no.)
>   POKE 23349, 0
>   POKE 23350, (step)
>   POKE 23351, 0

The above procedure works for all numbers between 0 and 255; if
you wish either parameter to be greater than 255 then the
procedure is different. For the first line number:

>   POKE 23348, (First line no.) −255 * INT ((first
>   line no.)/256)

POKE 23349, INT ((First line no.)/256)

Similarly, for the "step":

POKE 23350, (step) −256 * INT ((step)/256)
POKE 23351, INT ((step)/256)

In both cases, the renumbering is almost instant on entering

RANDOMIZE USR (start address of RENUMBER)

Be warned: do not use too big a first line number or step, or
the last line number may be greater than the limit of 9999.
This can have serious effects on your program when RUN, but you
can correct such a mistake by renumbering using more
appropriate parameters.

Here is the routine.

```
HEX.        ;RENUMBER LENGTH: 37 BYTES
            PROG    EQU     5C53H
            VARS    EQU     5C4BH
2A535C      START   LD      HL,(PROG)       ;HL=BEGINNING OF PROGRAM.
ED5B345B            LD      DE,(5B34H)      ;DE=FIRST NUMBER.
ED4B365B            LD      BC,(5B36H)      ;BC=STEP
D5                  PUSH    DE
EB          NXTLINE EX      DE,HL           ;HAVE WE REACHED THE
2A4B5C              LD      HL,(VARS)       ;VARIABLES AREA?
A7                  AND     A
ED52                SBC     HL,DE
EB                  EX      DE,HL
D1                  POP     DE
C8                  RET     Z               ;IF SO, RETURN TO BASIC.
72                  LD      (HL),D          ;INSERT NEW LINE NO.
23                  INC     HL
73                  LD      (HL),E
23                  INC     HL
EB                  EX      DE,HL
09                  ADD     HL,BC           ;ADD 'STEP' TO LINE NUMBER,
EB                  EX      DE,HL           ;GIVING NEXT NUMBER.
D5                  PUSH    DE
5E                  LD      E,(HL)          ;TAKE LENGTH OF CURRENT
23                  INC     HL              ;LINE.
56                  LD      D,(HL)
23                  INC     HL
19                  ADD     HL,DE           ;ADD LENGTH OF LINE TO
18E7                JR      NXTLINE         ;COUNTER. PROCEED TO
                    END                     ;RENUMBER NEXT LINE.
```

APPLICATION

You may already know that if the first line number of a program
is zero then it cannot be EDITed or removed without altering
the line number by POKEing it. If you make the "first line

number" in the renumber routine zero, and make the first line of your program a REM statement such as:

2 REM (c) David M. Webb, Hands off, pirates!!!!

then after renumbering the program, you will have a copyright line that cannot be EDITed.

CHAPTER 25
CASE CHANGE

This routine operates on the program rather than in it: it sets
all of the letters occurring in the BASIC listing to either
"Upper Case" (capitals) or "Lower Case" (small letters). This
can be useful if you want to make a ZX-printer LLIST more
legibly - just use the "Upper Case" mode and then LLIST away
with clear capitals to your heart's content.

CHOOSING UPPER OR LOWER CASE

You need just one POKE:

POKE 23356,   16 for Upper Case
              240 for Lower Case

The routine does not operate on anything after a REM statement
in a program line, in order to preserve any machine code that
you may have stored there. This can be used to added advantage
by temporarily inserting a REM statement before anything (such
as a PRINT statement) that you wish to 'protect' from the
action of the routine.

```
        HEX.        ;CASE CHANGE  LENGTH: 77 BYTES
                    PROG    EQU   5C53H
                    VARS    EQU   5C4BH
  2A535C            START   LD    HL,(PROG)     ;HAVE WE REACHED THE
  ED5B4B5C          NXTLINE LD    DE,(VARS)     ;END OF THE PROGRAM?
  EB                        EX    DE,HL
  A7                        AND   A
```

```
ED52                SBC     HL,DE       ;IF SO, THEN RETURN TO
C8                  RET     Z           ;BASIC.
EB                  EX      DE,HL
23                  INC     HL
23                  INC     HL
5E                  LD      E,(HL)      ;TAKE THE LENGTH OF
23                  INC     HL          ;THE LINE IN REGISTER DE.
56                  LD      D,(HL)
23                  INC     HL
7E          COLON   LD      A,(HL)      ;HAVE WE A REM STATEMENT?
FEEA                CP      0EAH        ;IF SO, THEN SKIP THIS LINE
2832                JR      Z,REMFND
0E00                LD      C,0
3A3C5B      NXTCHAR LD      A,(5B3CH)   ;LET B=PEEK 23356
47                  LD      B,A
C650                ADD     A,50H       ;IS THE CHARACTER IN THE
BE                  CP      (HL)        ;RANGE OF VALUES WHICH
3009                JR      NC,NOCHANG  ;MUST BE CHANGED FROM ONE
C61B                ADD     A,1BH       ;CASE TO THE OTHER?
BE                  CP      (HL)
3804                JR      C,NOCHANG   ;IF NOT THEN SKIP THIS...
7E                  LD      A,(HL)      ;CHANGE THE CASE OF THE
90                  SUB     B           ;CHARACTER.
90                  SUB     B
77                  LD      (HL),A
7E          NOCHANG LD      A,(HL)      ;MOVE ON TO THE NEXT
23                  INC     HL
1B                  DEC     DE
FE22                CP      22H         ;CHECK WHETHER WE'RE
2001                JR      NZ,NTQUOTE  ;INSIDE A SET OF QUOTES.
0C                  INC     C
CB41        NTQUOTE BIT     0,C         ;IF SO THEN NEXT CHARACTER,
20E2                JR      NZ,NXTCHAR  ;SINCE THE LINE CAN'T END
FE0E                CP      0EH         ;INSIDE A SET OF QUOTES.
2006                JR      NZ,NOTNUM   ;IF WE'VE FOUND A 5-BYTE
0605                LD      B,5         ;NUMBER THEN SKIP IT.
23          NXT1    INC     HL
1B                  DEC     DE
10FC                DJNZ    NXT1
FE3A        NOTNUM  CP      3AH         ;IF WE'VE FOUND A COLON
28CD                JR      Z,COLON     ;'SEPERATOR' THEN CHECK FOR
FE0D                CP      0DH         ;A REM AGAIN. IF NOT END OF
20C9                JR      NZ,COLON    ;LINE THEN NEXT CHARACTER.
19          REMFND  ADD     HL,DE       ;MOVE ON TO THE NEXT
18B6                JR      NXTLINE     ;PROGRAM LINE.
                    END
```

CHAPTER 26
FIND AND REPLACE

With this routine you can search through the BASIC program
(instantly, naturally) looking for a specific key word or
character and replacing it with a second byte. Thus two POKEs
are required:

        POKE 23352, CODE "(find character)"
        POKE 23353, CODE "(replace character)"

If you had used some character frequently as part of a screen
presentation, say "#" as the border for the screen, and wanted
to see what other characters would look like in the same place,
then it is far quicker to call up this routine to do the
"donkey work" rather than manually EDITing all of the
appropriate program lines.

EXAMPLE

change all the # symbols to & symbols in the program:

        POKE 23352, CODE "#"
        POKE 23353, CODE "&"
        LET L = USR ... (start address of routine)

PROGRAMMING CONSIDERATIONS

The routine ignores anything after a REM statement in a program
line in order to avoid mutilating any machine code the user may
have stored therein. 'Find and Replace' may be called from
within a program like most of the other routines in this book,

so you may like to use it to alter a set of PRINT statements during a program and then to go back over that section of the program, thereby varying the screen display by overprinting the 'found' characters with the 'replaced' ones. Remember also that you can change key words as well as characters, so the routine could be used to change SIN functions into COS in a trigonometrical graph – drawing program, or maybe to turn all your PRINTs into REMs if you wished to temporarily speed up the BASIC program.

Right then, here's the listing – don't forget to SAVE it when entered!

```
HEX.        ;FIND AND REPLACE  LENGTH: 81 BYTES
            PROG    EQU     5C53H
            VARS    EQU     5C4BH
2A535C      START   LD      HL,(PROG)       ;START AT THE BEGINNING.
ED5B4B5C    NXTLINE LD      DE,(VARS)       ;ARE WE AT THE END OF THE
EB                  EX      DE,HL           ;PROGRAM?
A7                  AND     A               ;BACK TO BASIC IF SO.
ED52                SBC     HL,DE
C8                  RET     Z
EB                  EX      DE,HL
23                  INC     HL
23                  INC     HL
5E                  LD      E,(HL)          ;TAKE THE LENGTH OF THE
23                  INC     HL              ;PROGRAM LINE.
56                  LD      D,(HL)
23                  INC     HL
7E          COLON   LD      A,(HL)          ;TAKE THE FIRST CHARACTER
FEEA                CP      0EAH            ;OF THE CURRENT STATEMENT.
                                            ;IS IT A REM? IF SO, THEN
282D                JR      Z,REMFND        ;SKIP TO THE NEXT LINE.
0E00                LD      C,0             ;IF C IS ODD THEN WE ARE
7E          NXTCHAR LD      A,(HL)          ;INSIDE QUOTE MARKS.
FE22                CP      22H             ;IS THIS CHARACTER A QUOTE?
2001                JR      NZ,NTQUOTE      ;IF SO, THEN CHANGE C FROM
0C                  INC     C               ;ODD TO EVEN OR VICE VERSA.
3A385B      NTQUOTE LD      A,(5B38H)       ;TAKE 'FIND' CHARACTER.
BE                  CP      (HL)            ;IS THE CURRENT CHARACTER A
2004                JR      NZ,NOFIND       ;'FIND' CHARACTER?
3A395B              LD      A,(5B39H)       ;IS SO, THEN REPLACE IT
77                  LD      (HL),A          ;WITH THE NEW VALUE.
7E          NOFIND  LD      A,(HL)          ;MOVE THE POINTERS TO THE
23                  INC     HL              ;NEXT CHARACTER.
1B                  DEC     DE
CB41                BIT     0,C             ;ARE WE IN QUOTES?
20E9                JR      NZ,NXTCHAR      ;IS SO, THEN NEXT CHARACTER
FE0E                CP      0EH             ;OTHERWISE CHECK FOR 5-BYTE
2006                JR      NZ,NOTNUM       ;FLOATING POINT NUMBERS AND
0605                LD      B,5             ;SKIP THEM WHEN FOUND.
23          NXT     INC     HL
1B                  DEC     DE
10FC                DJNZ    NXT             ;NOW CHECK FOR A COLON, AND
FE3A        NOTNUM  CP      3AH             ;IF FOUND, GO AND CHECK FOR
28D4                JR      Z,COLON         ;A REM. ARE WE AT THE END
```

```
FE0D              CP     0DH          ;OF THE LINE?
20D7              JR     NZ,NXTCHAR   ;IF NOT, NEXT CHARACTER...
188E              JR     NXTLINE      ;ELSE NEXT LINE.
ED4B385B  REMFND  LD     BC,(5B38H)   ;CHECK TO SEE IF THE REM
79                LD     A,C          ;SHOULD BE REPLACED, AND IF
BE                CP     (HL)         ;SO THEN DO SO.
2001              JR     NZ,NTRMFND
70                LD     (HL),B
19        NTRMFND ADD    HL,DE        ;SKIP ONTO THE NEXT LINE.
1882              JR     NXTLINE
                  END
```

CHAPTER 27
LINE DELETE

LINE DELETE is another of those utility routines which no
self-respecting BASIC programmer should be without. The short
routine allows you to delete any part of the program from one
line to all of it, instantly. Quite obviously to use the
routine we must specify two values; the first and last line
numbers to be deleted. Let's call the line we are deleting from
F, and the line we are deleting to, T. Then the correct
commands are:

                POKE 23357, F - 256 * INT (F/256)
                POKE 23358, INT (F/256)
                POKE 23359, T - 256 * INT (T/256)
                POKE 23360, INT (T/256)

Both values are included in the block deletion, and the second
and/or fourth POKEs may be omitted if the corresponding line
number is less than 256, since the number POKEd in would be
zero (do not omit the commands if you have previously POKEd in
non-zero values to 23358 or 23360!). To illustrate, if we were
to delete from line 25 to line 515 (both inclusive), then

                POKE 23357, 25: POKE 23359, 3: POKE 23360, 2.
                (note: 515 = (2 x 256) + 3)

Call the routine with   RANDOMIZE USR (start address)
                 or   LET A = USR (start address)

If you are deleting just one line (and either it hasn't
occurred to you to just type in the line number or you are

doing so from within a program) then the two values will be the same.

If you wish to delete from a line to the end of the program, then any line number greater than the last line number will also do for the second value. Hence:

POKE 23360, 40

will ensure that this is the case, since 40 x 256 = 10240, which is greater than the highest possible line number.

One useful sideline to this routine is that it can be used to save all variables onto tape in one go. Simply run the BASIC program so that all the variables are defined, then use the routine to DELETE the entire program. The variables will be unaffected, and these can then be saved just like a program with the SAVE command. To load them back into the same or any other program, type CLEAR if you want to get rid of the existing variables, then MERGE "(filename)" to load up the old variables from tape.

Here is the routine.

```
HEX.          ;LINE DELETE  LENGTH: 70 BYTES
              PROG    EQU   5C53H
              VARS    EQU   5C4BH
2A535C        START   LD    HL,(PROG)
ED4B3D5B              LD    BC,(5B3DH)    ;TAKE THE 'FROM' NUMBER.
EB            NXTLN   EX    DE,HL         ;HAVE WE REACHED THE BASIC
2A4B5C                LD    HL,(VARS)     ;VARIABLES?
A7                    AND   A
ED52                  SBC   HL,DE
C8                    RET   Z             ;RETURN TO BASIC IF SO.
EB                    EX    DE,HL
56                    LD    D,(HL)        ;TAKE A LINE NUMBER.
23                    INC   HL
5E                    LD    E,(HL)
EB                    EX    DE,HL         ;COMPARE IT WITH THE 'FROM'
ED42                  SBC   HL,BC         ;NUMBER.
EB                    EX    DE,HL
3008                  JR    NC,FOUNDFR    ;IF IT'S LESS THEN NEXT LINE
23                    INC   HL            ;OTHERWISE GO AND LOOK FOR
5E                    LD    E,(HL)        ;THE 'TO' LINE.
23                    INC   HL            ;TO FIND THE NEXT LINE, ADD
56                    LD    D,(HL)        ;THE LINE LENGTH TO THE
23                    INC   HL            ;POINTER.
19                    ADD   HL,DE
18E6                  JR    NXTLN         ;LOOP BACK.
E5            FOUNDFR PUSH  HL            ;STORE POINTER FOR 'FROM'
ED4B3F5B              LD    BC,(5B3FH)    ;START LOOKING FOR 'TO'
23            NXTLN2  INC   HL            ;MOVE POINTER TO NEXT
5E                    LD    E,(HL)        ;LINE NUMBER.
23                    INC   HL
56                    LD    D,(HL)
```

```
23                  INC     HL
19                  ADD     HL,DE
EB                  EX      DE,HL       ;HAVE WE REACHED THE
2A4B5C              LD      HL,(VARS)   ;VARIABLES?
A7                  AND     A
ED52                SBC     HL,DE
EB                  EX      DE,HL
280B                JR      Z,FOUNEND   ;IF SO, THEN GO AND DELETE,
56                  LD      D,(HL)      ;OTHERWISE TAKE THE NEXT
23                  INC     HL          ;LINE NUMBER.
5E                  LD      E,(HL)
EB                  EX      DE,HL
37                  SCF                 ;COMPARE IT WITH 'TO'
ED42                SBC     HL,BC       ;NUMBER.
EB                  EX      DE,HL       ;IF CURRENT NUMBER IS LESS
38E6                JR      C,NXTLN2    ;THAN OR EQUAL TO 'TO'
2B                  DEC     HL          ;NUMBER THEN NEXT LINE.
D1          FOUNEND POP     DE          ;NOW WE ARE READY TO DELETE
1B                  DEC     DE          ;WITH A JUMP TO THE ROM
C3E519              JP      19E5H       ;WHICH MOVES DOWN
                    END                 ;EVERYTHING ABOVE HL TO DE.
```

CHAPTER 28
FULL RENUMBER

I consider this routine to be one of the most useful pieces in this book. The program renumbers all of the BASIC program and correctly adjusts all non-computed GOTO, GOSUB, RUN, LLIST, LIST, RESTORE and SAVE... LINE commands. "Computed" commands such as GOTO a * b/c cannot be renumbered since the routine has no way of knowing what values any variables will take in the program.

Due to the sheer complexity of renumbering a program with its GOTOs and so on, this routine at 411 bytes is just over eleven times as long as its 37-byte counterpart in Chapter 24, which only affects the line numbers. Do not, however, be put off by the length; it is well worth the effort of typing in the code and can be invaluable when "tidying up" your BASIC listing or when you need to make room for more BASIC lines, due to all the line numbers in that area having been used up.

USING FULL RENUMBER

Before calling the routine with

        RANDOMIZE USR (start address)
    or LET A = USR (start address)

you must specify two parameters; the first new line number and the 'step' between line numbers, thus:

        POKE 23348, L - 256 * INT (L/256)
        POKE 23349, INT (L/256)

POKE 23350, S - 256 * INT (S/256)
POKE 23351, INT (S/256)

Where L is the first line number and S is the step.

You may omit the second and/or fourth commands if L and/or S are/is less than 256, as is usually the case, since the value of the POKEs would be zero.

Hence to renumber starting at line 10 in steps of 10,

POKE 23348, 10: POKE 23350, 10.

If you have particularly high line numbers being renumbered to particularly low numbers, then the overall length of the program may reduce, since

GOTO 9999 takes 3 bytes more than GOTO 9.

If the reverse case happens, the length will increase. So for safety's sake (i.e. to prevent an irreversible crash) the routine incorporates a fail-safe device which returns to BASIC with "Error 4 - Out of Memory" if there are less than 256 bytes of free memory. If you wish you can find out how much free memory you have by using the short routine in Chapter 23.

The routine ignores anything after a REM statement in a BASIC line, so machine code buffs can still store code in REM statements. If your program has a reference to a non-existent BASIC line then it will be altered to the nearest line number above that line, or to the next logical number if that line was the last in the program. That may seem a bit complex, so allow me to illustrate:

Renumbering this program from line 10 in steps of 10,

15 GOTO 31   becomes   10 GOTO 20
43 GOTO 999   20 GOTO 30

FULL RENUMBER works on about 2K of program per second, and incidentally uses the three spare bytes in the system variables area, so don't use them for your own purposes or you will lose your data!

```
HEX.        ;FULL RENUMBER  LENGTH: 411 BYTES
            STKEND  EQU     5C65H
            VARS    EQU     5C4BH
            PROG    EQU     5C53H
AF          MEMTEST XOR     A               ;CHECK FOR 256 SPARE
67                  LD      H,A             ;BYTES BETWEEN THE STACK
6F                  LD      L,A             ;POINTER AND END OF BASIC.
39                  ADD     HL,SP           ;IF THERE ISN'T THEN
ED4B655C            LD      BC,(STKEND)     ;RETURN TO BASIC...
ED42                SBC     HL,BC
BC                  CP      H
2002                JR      NZ,ROOM
```

```
CF                RST    8              ;WITH ERROR 4 - "OUT OF
03                DEFB   3              ;"MEMORY".
2A4B5C    ROOM    LD     HL,(VARS)      ;FIND THE FIRST BYTE
7E                LD     A,(HL)         ;AFTER THE BASIC PROGRAM,
32815C            LD     (5C81H),A      ;STORE IT AND THEN REPLACE
36FF              LD     (HL),0FFH      ;IT WITH AN FF MARKER.
2A535C            LD     HL,(PROG)      ;THE SEARCH FOR GOTO'S
7E        LOOP4   LD     A,(HL)         ;ETC. BEGINS. IF AT END OF
3C                INC    A              ;PROGRAM THEN JUMP TO
2850              JR     Z,SRCHEND      ;SRCHEND.
010000            LD     BC,0           ;BC HOLDS THE ALTERATION TO
23                INC    HL             ;THE LENGTH OF THE CURRENT
23                INC    HL             ;LINE, WHICH VARIES AS THE
23                INC    HL             ;ARGUMENTS OF GOTO'S ARE
E5                PUSH   HL             ;EXPANDED OR CONTRACTED.
C5                PUSH   BC
23        ENTRY20 INC    HL
7E        ENTRY4  LD     A,(HL)
0E00              LD     C,0            ;C KEEPS A CHECK ON QUOTES.
FEEA              CP     0EAH           ;CHECK FOR A REM. IF FOUND
283E              JR     Z,NXSRCLN      ;THEN SKIP CURRENT LINE.
08        LOOP3   EX     AF,AF'
7E                LD     A,(HL)         ;C IS INCREMENTED EVERY
23                INC    HL             ;TIME A QUOTATION MARK IS
FE22              CP     22H            ;DETECTED.
2001              JR     NZ,NTQUOTE
0C                INC    C
CB41      NTQUOTE BIT    0,C            ;IF C IS ODD DON'T CHECK
20F4              JR     NZ,LOOP3       ;FOR GOTO AS WE ARE INSIDE
FECA              CP     0CAH           ;QUOTE MARKS. CHECK FOR
2006              JR     NZ,ENTRY14     ;LINE.
08                EX     AF,AF'         ;IF LINE IS FOUND THEN
FEEE              CP     0EEH           ;UNLESS PREVIOUS BYTE WAS
205C              JR     NZ,ADJUST      ;INPUT, GO AND RENUMBER IT.
08                EX     AF,AF'
FE3A      ENTRY14 CP     3AH
28DF              JR     Z,ENTRY4
FEF0              CP     0F0H           ;CHECK FOR LIST.
2853              JR     Z,ADJUST
FE0E              CP     0EH            ;IF WE'VE FOUND A FLOATING-
2004              JR     NZ,NOTNUM      ;POINT NUMBER THEN SKIP ITS
110500            LD     DE,5           ;FIVE BYTES.
19                ADD    HL,DE
FEEC      NOTNUM  CP     0ECH           ;CHECK FOR GOTO.
2847              JR     Z,ADJUST
FEED              CP     0EDH           ;CHECK FOR GOSUB.
2843              JR     Z,ADJUST
FEE5              CP     0E5H           ;CHECK FOR RESTORE.
283F              JR     Z,ADJUST
FEF7              CP     0F7H           ;CHECK FOR RUN.
283B              JR     Z,ADJUST
FEE1              CP     0E1H           ;CHECK LLIST
2837              JR     Z,ADJUST
FE0D              CP     0DH            ;END OF LINE? IF NOT, THEN
20C2      LINK1   JR     NZ,LOOP3       ;ON TO THE NEXT CHARACTER.
```

```
C1          NXSRCLN POP   BC          ;BC=CHANGE TO LINE LENGTH.
E1                  POP   HL          ;HL=ADDRESS OF LINE LENGTH.
56                  LD    D,(HL)      ;TAKE OLD LINE LENGTH.
2B                  DEC   HL
5E                  LD    E,(HL)
EB                  EX    DE,HL
09                  ADD   HL,BC       ;ADD ALTERATION TO LINE
EB                  EX    DE,HL       ;LENGTH.
73                  LD    (HL),E      ;STORE NEW LINE LENGTH.
23                  INC   HL
72                  LD    (HL),D
23                  INC   HL
19                  ADD   HL,DE       ;MOVE ONTO NEXT LINE.
189F                JR    LOOP4
ED5B345B    SRCHEND LD    DE,(5B34H)  ;ALL RENUMBERING OF GOTO'S
ED4B365B            LD    BC,(5B36H)  ;ETC IS FINISHED, SO NOW
2A535C              LD    HL,(PROG)   ;ALTER ALL LINE NUMBERS.
7E          NXTLN2  LD    A,(HL)
3C                  INC   A           ;END OF PROGRAM?
2005                JR    NZ,NOSTOP   ;IF SO, THEN REPLACE FIRST
3A815C              LD    A,(5C81H)   ;BYTE AFTER BASIC PROGRAM
77                  LD    (HL),A      ;AND RETURN TO BASIC.
C9                  RET
72          NOSTOP  LD    (HL),D      ;STORE FIRST LINE NUMBER.
23                  INC   HL
73                  LD    (HL),E
23                  INC   HL
EB                  EX    DE,HL
09                  ADD   HL,BC       ;ADD THE 'STEP' TO THE LINE
EB                  EX    DE,HL       ;NUMBER.
D5                  PUSH  DE
5E                  LD    E,(HL)      ;TAKE THE LINE LENGTH, AND
23                  INC   HL          ;ADD IT TO THE POINTER.
56                  LD    D,(HL)
23                  INC   HL
19                  ADD   HL,DE
D1                  POP   DE          ;NOW MOVE ON TO ALTER THE
18E7                JR    NXTLN2      ;NEXT LINE NUMBER. THIS
7E          ADJUST  LD    A,(HL)      ;PART ALTERS GOTO'S ETC.
FE3A                CP    3AH         ;LOOK FOR THE BEGINNING OF
2882        CHEAT   JR    Z,ENTRY20   ;THE ASCII - CODED NUMBER
FE0D                CP    0DH         ;(STORED ONE DIGIT TO ONE
28C4                JR    Z,NXSRCLN   ;BYTE).
23                  INC   HL
FE20                CP    20H
38F2                JR    C,ADJUST
2B                  DEC   HL
22B05C              LD    (5CB0H),HL  ;STORE THIS ADDRESS.
0600                LD    B,0         ;B COUNTS UP THE NUMBER
7E          LOOP6   LD    A,(HL)      ;OF DIGITS OR COLOR BYTES
23                  INC   HL          ;IN THE ARGUMENT OF THE
FE0E                CP    0EH         ;GOTO. COUNT THEM UNTIL
282E                JR    Z,NUMFGUN   ;A FLOATING POINT NUMBER IS
FE20                CP    20H         ;FOUND, IGNORE COLOR CODES
38F6                JR    C,LOOP6     ;ETC., THEN IF THE CURRENT
```

127

```
FE3A                CP      3AH         ;BYTE ISN'T AN ASCII
3007                JR      NC,NOGO     ;NUMBER WE CANNOT RENUMBER
FE30                CP      30H         ;THE STATEMENT (NOGO).
3803                JR      C,NOGO
04                  INC     B
18EB                JR      LOOP6
7E      NOGO        LD      A,(HL)      ;LOOK ALONG THE BASIC
FE22                CP      22H         ;LINE UNTIL YOU FIND
2001                JR      NZ,NTQUOT2  ;A STATEMENT-SEPARATING
0C                  INC     C           ;COLON OR THE END-OF-LINE
CB41    NTQUOT2 BIT 0,C                 ;BYTE. IGNORE ANYTHING
2010                JR      NZ,NOTNUM2  ;INSIDE QUOTATION MARKS.
FE3A                CP      3AH
28CC                JR      Z,CHEAT
FE0D                CP      0DH
28C8                JR      Z,CHEAT
FE0E                CP      0EH
2004                JR      NZ,NOTNUM2
110500              LD      DE,5
19                  ADD     HL,DE
23      NOTNUM2 INC HL
18E3                JR      NOGO
1883    LINK2       JR      LINK1       ;PART OF A 3-STEP RELATIVE
110500  NUMFOUN     LD      DE,5        ;JUMP FROM END OF ROUTINE.
19                  ADD     HL,DE       ;A FLOATING-PT. NUMBER HAS
7E                  LD      A,(HL)      ;BEEN FOUND. IF IT'S NOT
FE0D                CP      0DH         ;FOLLOWED BY A COLON OR
2804                JR      Z,OK        ;END-OF-LINE BYTE THEN WE
FE3A                CP      3AH         ;CANNOT RENUMBER THE
20D4                JR      NZ,NOGO     ;CURRENT STATEMENT.
2B      OK          DEC     HL          ;TAKE THE LINE NUMBER
2B                  DEC     HL          ;REFERRED TO IN THE CURRENT
C5                  PUSH    BC          ;STATEMENT FROM ITS FIVE-
E5                  PUSH    HL          ;BYTE FORM.
56                  LD      D,(HL)
2B                  DEC     HL
5E                  LD      E,(HL)
ED4B345B            LD      BC,(5B34H)  ;BC=FIRST NEW LINE NUMBER.
C5                  PUSH    BC
2A535C              LD      HL,(PROG)   ;CALCULATE THE NEW LINE
7E      NXT9        LD      A,(HL)      ;NUMBER BY ADDING THE
3C                  INC     A           ;STEP TO THE FIRST LINE
281D                JR      Z,CNTDOWN   ;NUMBER AND WORKING
46                  LD      B,(HL)      ;THROUGH THE LISTING UNTIL
23                  INC     HL          ;WE FIND A LINE NUMBER
4E                  LD      C,(HL)      ;GREATER THAN OR EQUAL
23                  INC     HL          ;TO THE NUMBER REFERRED
EB                  EX      DE,HL       ;TO IN THE CURRENT STATE-
E5                  PUSH    HL          ;MENT.
37                  SCF
ED42                SBC     HL,BC
E1                  POP     HL
3811                JR      C,CNTDOWN
EB                  EX      DE,HL
E3                  EX      (SP),HL
```

```
ED4B365B        LD      BC,(5B36H)
09              ADD     HL,BC
E3              EX      (SP),HL
4E              LD      C,(HL)
23              INC     HL
46              LD      B,(HL)
23              INC     HL
09              ADD     HL,BC
18E1            JR      NXT9
18C1    LINK3   JR      LINK2           ;PART OF A 3-STEP RELATIVE
D1      CNTDOWN POP     DE              ;JUMP HAVING CALCULATED
E1              POP     HL              ;THE NEW LINE NUMBER FOR
72              LD      (HL),D          ;THE GOTO, STORE IT IN
2B              DEC     HL              ;IT'S FIVE BYTE FORM.
73              LD      (HL),E
3E01            LD      A,1             ;NOW CALCULATE THE
21F6FF          LD      HL,0FFF6H       ;NUMBER OF DIGITS IN
19              ADD     HL,DE           ;THE NEW LINE NUMBER,
300F            JR      NC,STOPCNT      ;THE RESULT BEING STORED
3C              INC     A               ;IN A.
219CFF          LD      HL,0FF9CH
19              ADD     HL,DE
3008            JR      NC,STOPCNT
3C              INC     A
2118FC          LD      HL,0FC18H
19              ADD     HL,DE
3001            JR      NC,STOPCNT
3C              INC     A
C1      STOPCNT POP     BC              ;B=# OF CHARS IN OLD NUMBER
E1              POP     HL              ;HL=ALTERATION TO CURRENT
                                        ;LINE LENGTH.
F5              PUSH    AF              ;STACK NO. OF CHARACTERS.
D5              PUSH    DE              ;STACK NEW LINE NO.
ED5BB05C        LD      DE,(5CB0H)      ;DE=ADDRESS OF ASCII CODED
D5              PUSH DE                 ;LINE NUMBER.
90              SUB     B               ;IF THE NEW LINE NUMBER
281C            JR      Z,NOCHANG       ;HAS MORE OR LESS DIGITS
4F              LD      C,A             ;THAN THE OLD THEN WE
D5              PUSH    DE              ;MUST MOVE THE REST OF
3809            JR      C,DOWN          ;THE BASIC PROGRAM AND
0600            LD      B,0             ;VARIABLES UP OR DOWN THE
09              ADD     HL,BC           ;MEMORY BY UP TO 3 BYTES.
E3              EX      (SP),HL         ;CARE IS TAKEN TO ENSURE
CD5516          CALL    1655H           ;THAT ALL OF THE SYSTEM
180E            JR      PLUGIN          ;VARAIBLE POINTERS ARE
2F      DOWN    CPL                     ;ADJUSTED ACCORDINGLY. THE
3C              INC     A               ;ROUTINE AT 1655H IN THE
5F              LD      E,A             ;ORIGINAL ROM MAKES BC
1600            LD      D,0             ;SPACES FROM HL.
06FF            LD      B,0FFH          ;THE ROUTINE AT 19E5H
09              ADD     HL,BC           ;MOVES ALL PARTS OF BASIC
E3              EX      (SP),HL         ;ABOVE HL DOWN FROM HL
EB              EX      DE,HL           ;TO DE. BOTH ROUTINES CALL
19              ADD     HL,DE           ;A ROUTINE WHICH ADJUSTS
```

```
CDE519              CALL  19E5H       ;THE POINTERS.
E1       PLUGIN  POP   HL
C1       NOCHANG POP   BC            ;CALCULATE THE ASCII CODE
D1               POP   DE            ;OF THE NEW NUMBER. DECIDE
F1               POP   AF            ;WHERE TO START, DEPENDING
E5               PUSH  HL            ;ON HOW MANY DIGITS
210100           LD    HL,1          ;THERE ARE. UNITS,
3D               DEC   A
2810             JR    Z,LOCKDON
E5               PUSH  HL
2E0A             LD    L,10          ;TENS,
3D               DEC   A
280A             JR    Z,LOCKDON
E5               PUSH  HL
2E64             LD    L,64H         ;HUNDREDS,
3D               DEC   A
2804             JR    Z,LOCKDON
E5               PUSH  HL
21E803           LD    HL,03E8H      ;THOUSANDS.
EB       LOCKDON EX    DE,HL         ;A STARTS WITH THE CODE OF
3E2F     NXTCHAR LD    A,2FH         ;"0" MINUS ONE.
A7               AND   A             ;SUBTRACT THE POWER OF TEN
ED52     LOOP10  SBC   HL,DE         ;FROM LINE NUMBER UNTIL
3C               INC   A             ;THERE IS A CARRY, INCRE-
30FB             JR    NC,LOOP10     ;MENTING THE DIGIT EACH
19               ADD   HL,DE         ;TIME. ADD THE POWER OF 10.
02               LD    (BC),A        ;STORE THE CURRENT DIGIT.
03               INC   BC            ;IF DE=1 THEN THE
1D               DEC   E             ;RENUMBERING IS COMPLETE
2006             JR    NZ,HOPIT      ;AND WE CAN MOVE ON TO THE
60               LD    H,B           ;NEXT STATEMENT IN THE
69               LD    L,C           ;PROGRAM, CLEARING C TO
4B               LD    C,E           ;INDICATE THAT WE ARE NOT
1C               INC   E             ;IN QUOTATION MARKS. MAKE A
18BB             JR    LINK3         ;THREE-STEP RELATIVE JUMP.
D1       HOPIT   POP   DE            ;MOVE ON TO PRODUCE NEXT
18E9             JR    NXTCHAR       ;DIGIT.
                 END
```

CHAPTER 29
THE SPECTRUM GETS A TRACE FUNCTION

This routine imitates the TRACE function often found on other
microcomputers. When a BASIC program is being run, TRACE will
automatically display the number of the line currently being
interpreted at the top right-hand corner of the screen. In
order to make the number stand out against whatever else is on
the screen, the routine prints the number in inverse video.
TRACE can be of great use when debugging your programs, as it
allows you to follow the progress of the machine through your
masterpiece without having to stop it.

For technical reasons, I have written two versions of TRACE;
one for the 16K Spectrum and one for the larger machine. These
routines are unique in this book in that they must be located
at a specific address, that is to say they are LOCATION
DEPENDENT.

To "turn on" the TRACE function, we use one USR call. To turn
it off, we use another seperate one. The addresses of these
calls are different for the two routines.

In order to enter the hex. code, first select option 7 of
HEXAID and clear the machine code area. Now select option 1
("write a routine"). In response to the "length of routine"
prompt, enter 118 for TRACE 48, or 252 for TRACE 16. The latter
number is not a misprint. Although TRACE 16 is physically only
114 bytes long, we must enter 252 in order to position the
routine at the correct start address. Now enter the hex. code
in the usual way.

Here is a table of start addresses and lengths for the SAVE option of HEXAID, together with the commands to turn the TRACE ON and OFF. Once the routine has been turned on, the current line number will be displayed automatically whenever a program is running. Note that you may turn TRACE on or off from within a program.

	TRACE 16	TRACE 48
Start address	32348	65250
Length	114	118
Command for TRACE ON	RANDOMIZE USR 32448	RANDOMIZE USR 65250
Command for TRACE OFF	RANDOMIZE USR 32455	RANDOMIZE USR 65257
Printing in INVERSE VIDEO	POKE 32441, 47	POKE 65361, 47
Printing in TRUE VIDEO	POKE 32441, 0	POKE 65361, 0

Now the the routines: make sure you get the right one!

```
HEX.         ;TRACE 16  LENGTH: See bottom paragraph on page 131.
FF      ENTRY   RST   38H          ;CALL THE USUAL INTERRUPT
F5              PUSH  AF           ;ROUTINE. STORE REGISTERS.
E5              PUSH  HL
2A455C          LD    HL,(23621)   ;SYSTEM VARIABLE.PPC.
24              INC   H            ;IF HI-BYTE=HEX FF THEN
2841            JR    Z,OUT        ;PROGRAM ISN'T BEING RUN
C5              PUSH  BC           ;SO JUMP TO THE END
D5              PUSH  DE           ;OF THE ROUTINE.
25              DEC   H
AF              XOR   A
47              LD    B,A
4F              LD    C,A
11E803          LD    DE,1000      ;CALCULATE THE THOUSAND'S
ED52    NXT1    SBC   HL,DE        ;DIGIT.
3C              INC   A
30FB            JR    NC,NXT1
19              ADD   HL,DE
3D              DEC   A
E5              PUSH  HL
CDA97E          CALL  PRNTNUM      ;PRINT IT.
E1              POP   HL
116400          LD    DE,100       ;CALCULATE THE
AF              XOR   A            ;HUNDRED'S DIGIT.
ED52    NXT2    SBC   HL,DE
3C              INC   A
30FB            JR    NC,NXT2
19              ADD   HL,DE
3D              DEC   A
0E01            LD    C,1
E5              PUSH  HL
CDA97E          CALL  PRNTNUM      ;PRINT IT.
E1              POP   HL
110A00          LD    DE,10        ;CALCULATE THE
7D              LD    A,L          ;TEN'S DIGIT.
```

```
93          NXT3    SUB     E
14                  INC     D
30FC                JR      NC,NXT3
15                  DEC     D
83                  ADD     A,E
67                  LD      H,A
E5                  PUSH    HL
0E02                LD      C,2
7A                  LD      A,D
CDA97E              CALL    PRNTNUM         ;PRINT IT.
F1                  POP     AF              ;WE'RE LEFT WITH THE
0E03                LD      C,3             ;UNITS:-PRINT THEM
CDA97E              CALL    PRNTNUM
D1                  POP     DE              ;RESTORE THE REGISTERS
C1                  POP     BC
E1          OUT     POP     HL
F1                  POP     AF
C9                  RET                     ;RETURN FROM INTERRUPT.
211C40      PRNTNUM LD      HL,401CH        ;THE A REGISTER
09                  ADD     HL,BC           ;HOLD THE DIGIT TO BE
87                  ADD     A,A             ;PRINTED, THE C REGISTER
87                  ADD     A,A             ;HOLDS THE NUMBER OF
87                  ADD     A,A             ;THE DIGIT (0 TO 3).
EB                  EX      DE,HL
4F                  LD      C,A
21803D              LD      HL,3D80H
09                  ADD     HL,BC
0608                LD      B,8
7E          NXT     LD      A,(HL)
2F                  CPL                     ;THIS BYTE DETERMINES
12                  LD      (DE),A          ;INVERSE (CPL) OR TRUE
23                  INC     HL              ;(NOP) VIDEO.
14                  INC     D
10F9                DJNZ    NXT
C9                  RET
3E28        TRON    LD      A,28H           ;TRACE ON BY VECTORING
ED47                LD      I,A             ;THE INTERRUPTS VIA
ED5E                IM      2               ;28FF, WHERE BYTES
C9                  RET                     ;5C AND 7E ARE STORED.
ED56        TROFF   IM      1               ;TRACE OFF BY RESTORING
3E3F                LD      A,3FH           ;I TO ITS ORIGINAL VALUE
ED47                LD      I,A             ;AND RESELECTING
C9                  RET                     ;INTERRUPT MODE 1.
                    END
```

```
HEX.        ;TRACE 48  LENGTH: 118 BYTES
3EFE        TRON    LD      A,0FEH          ;TRACE ON BY VECTORING
ED47                LD      I,A             ;THE INTERRUPTS VIA
ED5E                IM      2               ;FEFF TO FEF0, LABEL
C9                  RET                     ;ENTRY.
ED56        TROFF   IM      1               ;TRACE OFF BY RESTORING
3E3F                LD      A,3FH           ;I TO 3F AND RESELECTING
ED47                LD      I,A             ;INTERRUPT MODE 1.
C9                  RET
```

```
FF          ENTRY   RST     38H         ;CALL THE USUAL INTERRUPT
F5                  PUSH    AF          ;ROUTINE. STORE REGISTERS.
E5                  PUSH    HL
2A455C              LD      HL,(23621)  ;SYSTEM VARIABLE PPC.
24                  INC     H           ;IF HI-BYTE=HEX FF THEN
2845                JR      Z,OUT       ;PROGRAM ISN'T BEING RUN
C5                  PUSH    BC          ;SO JUMP TO THE END
D5                  PUSH    DE          ;OF THE ROUTINE.
25                  DEC     H
AF                  XOR     A
1802                JR      HOP         ;HOP AROUND THE INTERRUPT
F0FE                DEFW    0FEF0H      ;VECTOR ADDRESS.
47          HOP     LD      B,A
4F                  LD      C,A
11E803              LD      DE,1000     ;CALCULATE THE THOUSAND'S
ED52        NXT1    SBC     HL,DE       ;DIGIT.
3C                  INC     A
30FB                JR      NC,NXT1
19                  ADD     HL,DE
3D                  DEC     A
E5                  PUSH    HL
CD41FF              CALL    PRNTNUM     ;PRINT IT.
E1                  POP     HL
116400              LD      DE,100      ;CALCULATE THE
AF                  XOR     A           ;HUNDRED'S DIGIT.
ED52        NXT2    SBC     HL,DE
3C                  INC     A
30FB                JR      NC,NXT2
19                  ADD     HL,DE
3D                  DEC     A
0E01                LD      C,1
E5                  PUSH    HL
CD41FF              CALL    PRNTNUM     ;PRINT IT.
E1                  POP     HL
110A00              LD      DE,10       ;CALCULATE THE
7D                  LD      A,L         ;TEN'S DIGIT.
93          NXT3    SUB     E
14                  INC     D
30FC                JR      NC,NXT3
15                  DEC     D
83                  ADD     A,E
67                  LD      H,A
E5                  PUSH    HL
0E02                LD      C,2
7A                  LD      A,D
CD41FF              CALL    PRNTNUM     ;PRINT IT.
F1                  POP     AF          ;WE'RE LEFT WITH THE
0E03                LD      C,3         ;UNITS:-PRINT THEM
CD41FF              CALL    PRNTNUM
D1                  POP     DE          ;RESTORE THE REGISTERS
C1                  POP     BC
E1          OUT     POP     HL
F1                  POP     AF
C9                  RET                 ;RETURN FROM INTERRUPT.
211C40      PRNTNUM LD      HL,401CH    ;THE A REGISTER
```

```
09                ADD    HL,BC      ;HOLDS THE DIGIT TO BE
87                ADD    A,A        ;PRINTED, THE C REGISTER
87                ADD    A,A        ;HOLDS THE NUMBER OF
87                ADD    A,A        ;THE DIGIT (0 TO 3).
EB                EX     DE,HL
4F                LD     C,A
21803D            LD     HL,3D80H
09                ADD    HL,BC
0608              LD     B,8
7E       NXT      LD     A,(HL)
2F                CPL               ;THIS BYTE DETERMINES
12                LD     (DE),A     ;INVERSE (CPL) OR TRUE
23                INC    HL         ;(NOP) VIDEO.
14                INC    D
10F9              DJNZ   NXT
C9                RET               ;END OF PRINT ROUTINE.
                  END
```

A NOTE FOR THE TECHNICALLY MINDED

Due to the phenomenon of picture break-up that occurs when the
interrupt vector holds values between hex. 40 and 7F, it is
necessary to vector interrupts under mode two via an address
less than 4000H (i.e. in the ROM) on a 16K Spectrum. The data
bus on a Spectrum always holds hex. FF at the time of an
interrupt. This leaves us with a choice of 63 different
interrupt tables each with one address in them. Of these, only
seven are in the 16K RAM area, one of which is in the screen.
Of the remaining six addresses, the only one remotely near the
32K boundary is that stored at addresses 28FF and 2900 hex. The
value of this is hex. 7E5C, which is where I have put the entry
point of TRACE 16.

ENHANCING YOUR PROGRAMS

CHAPTER 30
GEOGRAPHIC KEYBOARD SCANS

GEOGRAPHIC KEYBOARD SCANS

If you have read page 160 of the Spectrum Manual then you will
know that it is possible to read the keyboard using the IN
function. The great advantage of this against the INKEY$
function is that you can detect the depression of more than one
key at any one time. In this way it is possible to combine
(say) two direction keys to produce a diagonal movement in a
game rather than presenting the player with the 'finger
gymnastics' task of using eight different direction keys.

The one problem with IN is that it can be rather slow and
clumsy to use, especially if you are reading only one key in a
given 'half-row' of five keys. By now you will probably have
guessed that machine code offers the solution: in fact IN and
OUT are the most similar words in Spectrum BASIC to their
counterparts in assembly language, namely the IN and OUT
instructions on which they are based.

I have included in this chapter a suite of five machine-code
keyboard routines to suit your every programming need. You use
them with a command – such as:

LET A = USR (start address)

It is important to use LET rather than RANDOMIZE, since the
value that A takes will be the number returned from the routine
and can then be used in IF... THEN statements and so on.

The routines are called 'geographic' because they attempt to

lay out the directions in corresponding areas of the keyboard,
e.g. the top row of the keys can be used to move upwards.

The first routine, GEOSCAN1, offers the four directions
(combinable to eight) and a keyboard layout like this:

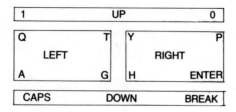

The numbers returned are as follows:

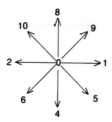

GEOSCAN1 is ideal for Pac-Man type games!

```
HEX.          ;GEOSCAN1 LENGTH: 48 BYTES
01001F    START   LD   BC,1F00H      ;B=MASK ON INPUT PORT,
3E9F              LD   A,9FH         ;C WILL HOLD THE RETURN
DBFE              IN   A,(0FEH)      ;VALUE.
2F                CPL                ;CHECK FOR 'RIGHT'....
A0                AND  B
2803              JR   Z,NTRIGHT
0C                INC  C             ;IF SO THEN LET C=1 AND
180A              JR   NOTLEFT       ;DON'T CHECK FOR 'LEFT'.
3EF9      NTRIGHT LD   A,0F9H        ;CHECK FOR 'LEFT'.
DBFE              IN   A,(0FEH)
2F                CPL,
A0                AND  B
2802              JR   Z,NOTLEFT     ;IF LEFT THEN LET C=2
CBC9              SET  1,C
3E7E      NOTLEFT LD   A,7EH         ;CHECK FOR 'DOWN'.
DBFE              IN   A,(0FEH)
2F                CPL
A0                AND  B
0600              LD   B,0
2803              JR   Z,NOTDOWN
```

```
0022 CBD1   00330        SET  2,C       ;IF 'DOWN' THEN C=C+4,
0024 C9     00340        RET            ;AND RETURN TO BASIC.
0025 3EE7   00350 NOTDOWN LD  A,0E7H    ;OTHERWISE CHECK FOR
0027 DBFE   00360        IN   A,(0FEH)  ;'UP' ...
0029 2F     00370        CPL
002A E61F   00380        AND  1FH
002C C8     00390        RET  Z         ;AND IF AN 'UP' KEY IS
002D CBD9   00400        SET  3,C       ;PRESSED THEN LET C=C+8.
002F C9     00410        RET            ;RETURN TO BASIC.
0000        00420        END
```

Note that in all of the GEOSCAN routines, I have given 'right'
priority over 'left', and 'down' priority over 'up'.

The second GEOSCAN routine checks for just two sets of keys; in
doing this it divides the keys vertically down the middle and
then checks each of the two halves for a key-press. This
routine would be at its best in a 'Breakout'-type game.

Layout   Values

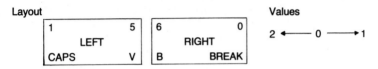

It should be realised at this point that the directions that I
have attached to the values returned are entirely arbitrary;
you could, for example, equally use the values from GEOSCAN2 to
mean "turn anticlockwise" and "turn clockwise", or in a
calculating program "print subtotals" and "don't print
subtotals".

```
HEX.        ;GEOSCAN2 LENGTH: 25 BYTES
010000  START LD  BC,0      ;BC HOLDS THE RETURN
3E0F          LD  A,0FH     ;VALUE. CHECK THE RIGHT-
DBFE          IN  A,(0FEH)  ;HAND HALF OF THE KEY-
2F            CPL           ;BOARD.
E61F          AND 1FH
2802          JR  Z,NTRIGHT
0C            INC C         ;RETURN THE VALUE 1 IF
C9            RET           ;PRESSED.
3EF0    NTRIGHT LD A,0F0H   ;CHECK THE LEFT-HAND
DBFE          IN  A,(0FEH)  ;SIDE.
2F            CPL
E61F          AND 1FH
C8            RET Z         ;RETURN IF NO KEY PRESS.
CBC9          SET 1,C       ;OTHERWISE RETURN VALUE
C9            RET           ;2 IN BC TO BASIC.
              END
```

The logical counterpart to GEOSCAN2 is (you guessed it) a
routine which divides the keyboard into halves horizontally
and is ideal for any game involving only vertical control, such

as control of the up-down bat movement in a 'squash' game. Here
are the layout and values...

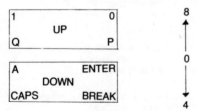

... and here is the routine. As usual, call it with

LET A = USR (start address)

```
HEX.            ;GEOSCAN3 LENGTH: 26 BYTES
010000    START  LD    BC,0        ;BC HOLDS THE RETURN
3E3C             LD    A,3CH       ;VALUE. CHECK THE BOTTOM
DBFE             IN    A,(0FEH)    ;HALF OF THE KEYBOARD.
2F               CPL
E61F             AND   1FH
2803             JR    Z,NOTDOWN
CBD1             SET   2,C         ;RETURN THE VALUE OF 4
C9               RET               ;IF PRESSED.
3EC3    NOTDOWN  LD    A,0C3H      ;CHECK THE TOP HALF.
DBFE             IN    A,(0FEH)
2F               CPL
E61F             AND   1FH
C8               RET   Z           ;RETURN IF NO KEY PRESS.
CBD9             SET   3,C         ;OTHERWISE RETURN VALUE
C9               RET               ;8 IN BC TO BASIC.
                 END
```

If you are a space-invader fan then this next keyboard routine
is the one for you. It uses the bottom row of the keyboard for
a 'fire' control and divides the other three rows down the
middle, as before, into left and right laser-base control
regions.

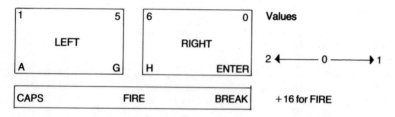

Note that this gives you the ability to detect movement and
FIRE controls simultaneously (e.g. FIRE and LEFT gives value
18).

```
HEX.        ;GEOSCAN4  LENGTH: 36 BYTES
01001F   START  LD    BC,1F00H     ;B=MASK ON INPUT PORT,
3E8F            LD    A,8FH        ;C WILL HOLD THE RETURN
DBFE            IN    A,(0FEH)     ;VALUE. CHECK FOR 'RIGHT'
2F              CPL                ;CONTROL.
A0              AND   B
2803            JR    Z,NTRIGHT
0C              INC   C            ;IF PRESSED, THEN LET C=1
180A            JR    NOTLEFT      ;AND DON'T CHECK 'LEFT'.
3EF1     NTRIGHT LD   A,0F1H       ;CHECK FOR 'LEFT'.
DBFE            IN    A,(0FEH)
2F              CPL
A0              AND   B
2802            JR    Z,NOTLEFT    ;IF PRESSED, THEN LET
CBC9            SET   1,C          ;C=2
3E7E     NOTLEFT LD   A,7EH        ;CHECK THE BOTTOM
DBFE            IN    A,(0FEH)     ;ROW (FIRE).
2F              CPL
A0              AND   B
0600            LD    B,0          ;IF PRESSED THEN ADD
C8              RET   Z            ;16 TO THE VALUE AND
CBE1            SET   4,C          ;RETURN IT IN BC TO
C9              RET                ;BASIC.
                END
```

For the final GEOSCAN routine I have used a layout similar to
that found on many popular arcade games for the ZX-Spectrum,
including Melbourne House's No. 1-selling "Penetrator" game for
the 48K machine. The controls are:

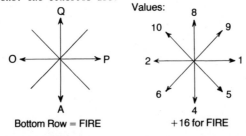

Bottom Row = FIRE   +16 for FIRE

... and here is the routine.

```
HEX.        ;GEOSCAN5  LENGTH: 49 BYTES
010000   START  LD    BC,0         ;BC WILL HOLD THE RET-
3EDF            LD    A,0DFH       ;URN VALUE. CHECK THE
DBFE            IN    A,(0FEH)     ;"P" KEY.
1F              RRA
3803            JR    C,NTRIGHT
0C              INC   C            ;IF PRESSED, THEN BC=1, AND
1805            JR    NOTLEFT      ;DON'T CHECK FOR 'LEFT'.
1F       NTRIGHT RRA               ;CHECK "Q" KEY.
3802            JR    C,NOTLEFT
CBC9            SET   1,C          ;IF PRESSED THEN BC=2
3EFD     NOTLEFT LD   A,0FDH       ;CHECK THE "A" KEY.
```

141

```
DBFE                IN      A,(OFEH)
1F                  RRA
3804                JR      C,NOTDOWN    ;IF PRESSED THEN BC=BC+4,
CBD1                SET     2,C          ;AND DON'T CHECK "UP".
1809                JR      NOTUP
3EFB     NOTDOWN LD         A,0FBH       ;CHECK THE "Q" KEY. IF
DBFE                IN      A,(OFEH)     ;PRESSED, THEN BC=BC+8.
1F                  RRA
3802                JR      C,NOTUP
CBD9                SET     3,C
3E7E     NOTUP   LD         A,7EH
DBFE                IN      A,(OFEH)     ;CHECK FOR THE BOTTOM
2F                  CPL                  ;"FIRE" ROW.
E61F                AND     1FH          ;IF IT IS PRESSED THEN
C8                  RET     Z            ;ADD 16 TO RESULT
CBE1                SET     4,C
C9                  RET                  ;RETURN TO BASIC.
                    END
```

CHAPTER 31
SUPERPLOT 256 x 192

This routine lets you plot on the bottom two lines of the screen as well as the rest of it. I have used a new system of coordinates; the top-left corner of the screen is now (0,0), thus:

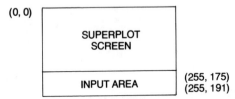

(0, 0)

SUPERPLOT
SCREEN

INPUT AREA

(255, 175)
(255, 191)

To use SUPERPLOT to plot a point (x,y):

POKE 23677, X : POKE 23678, Y
RANDOMIZE USR [start address]

The routine follows all the usual rules for the current INVERSE and OVER values, and does not affect the colour bytes. Here it is:

```
HEX.          ;SUPERPLOT 256*192 LENGTH: 68 BYTES
2A7D5C   START  LD   HL,(5C7DH)   ;SYSTEM VARIABLE COORDS
7C              LD   A,H          ;L=X, H=Y
E6C0            AND  0C0H         ;LOCATE THE RIGHT
0F              RRCA              ;THIRD OF THE SCREEN
0F              RRCA
```

```
0F                RRCA
C640              ADD     A,40H
57                LD      D,A
7C                LD      A,H
E607              AND     07H             ;NOW FIND THE RIGHT ROW.....
82                ADD     A,D
57                LD      D,A
7C                LD      A,H             ;...OF THE RIGHT LINE
87                ADD     A,A             ;ON THE SCREEN
87                ADD     A,A
E6E0              AND     0E0H
5F                LD      E,A
7D                LD      A,L             ;FIND THE RIGHT COLUMN.
E6F8              AND     0F8H            ;NOW WE HAVE THE
0F                RRCA                    ;ADDRESS OF THE BYTE OF
0F                RRCA                    ;THE SCREEN TO BE
0F                RRCA                    ;ALTERED
B3                OR      E
5F                LD      E,A
EB                EX      DE,HL
0EFE              LD      C,0FEH          ;C HOLDS THE MASK
AF                XOR     A               ;FOR THE OLD BYTE.
FDCB575E          BIT     3,(IY+57H)      ;A HOLDS THE NEW BIT.
2001              JR      NZ,HOP          ;IY+57H=SYSTEM
3C                INC     A               ;VARIABLE P FLAG. BIT
57        HOP     LD      D,A             ;3 SIGNIFIES INVERSE
7B                LD      A,E             ;VALUE.
E607              AND     07H
47                LD      B,A
04                INC     B
79                LD      A,C
CB0A      NXT     RRC     D               ;SHIFT THE MASK (NOW
0F                RRCA                    ;IN A) AND THE NEW
10FB              DJNZ    NXT             ;BIT TO THE RIGHT POINT.
FDCB574E          BIT     1,(IY+57H)      ;BIT 1 OF P FLAG IS THE
2004              JR      NZ,OVER         ;OVER VALUE.
A6                AND     (HL)            ;PLOT OVER 0,X,Y.
B2                OR      D
77                LD      (HL),A
C9                RET                     ;RETURN TO BASIC.
7A        OVER    LD      A,D             ;PLOT OVER 1,X,Y.
AE                XOR     (HL)
77                LD      (HL),A
C9                RET                     ;RETURN TO BASIC
                  END
```

The demonstration below will plot a sine curve, using the full screen. Don't forget to alter the start address in line 30.

Line 80 forms an infinite loop in order to stop the computer overwriting the bottom two lines of the screen with a report code. Press BREAK to end this.

```
   10 REM SUPERPLOT DEMO
   20 REM © DAVID M.WEBB, 1983
   30 LET PLOT=65000: REM START A
DDRESS
   40 FOR A=0 TO 255
   50 POKE 23677,A: POKE 23678,96
-95*SIN (A*PI/128): REM SET X,Y
COORDINATES
   60 RANDOMIZE USR PLOT
   70 NEXT A
   80 GO TO 80
```

CHAPTER 32
TAPE RELAY

The tiny Z-80 microprocessor or CPU (Central Processing Unit) at the heart of your Spectrum is linked to the outside world by what are known as INput and OUTput ports. In the case of the Spectrum these take the form of the EAR socket and keyboard (IN) and the MIC socket, television, loudspeaker (well O.K., quiet BEEPer) and printer (OUT).

These ports can be accessed from BASIC by use of the aptly-named IN and OUT commands (see Chapter 23, page 159 of the manual) but unfortunately BASIC cannot provide a fast enough sampling or "reading" rate to relay sound IN through the ear socket and OUT through the speaker. This can be demonstrated thus:

```
10 REM This relay program is too slow
20 OUT 254, 0: OUT 254, INT ((IN 254)/4): GOTO 20
```

You will find that although the above program produces a series of "clicks" when you play your favourite Beethoven sonata at full volume and high tone through the EAR socket, they are not frequent enough to produce a recognisable sound. For this we have to resort to machine code, because it "refreshes the ports at a speed that other languages cannot reach!"

The following routine was written to provide the highest possible sampling rate, in an effort to achieve the best possible "relay" sound quality. As a result the EAR port is "read" approximately once every 17 microseconds (a microsecond is a millionth of a second) and this produces a sampling rate

of about 57000 times per second (57 Kilohertz). For reasons
best known to the hardware enthusiasts amongst you, the signal
output to the speaker can be very weak. I find the best sound
reproduction is achieved as follows:

1. Disconnect the lead from the "MIC" socket on the tape
recorder to that at the back of the Spectrum — this prevents
'feed-back' distorting the sound;

2. Connect the lead between the EAR sockets of the two devices
in the normal fashion;

3. Put the volume control on maximum setting, and if you have
a "tone" control then do likewise for that (the reason for the
latter adjustment is that the circuitry inside the computer
incorporates a "Schmitt trigger" which does wonders for
filtering out background noise when LOADing but does have a
habit of removing "low-tone" sound).

Before we go any further I'd better let you have the routine.

```
HEX.          ;TAPE RELAY  LENGTH: 27 BYTES
F3       START  DI                    ;STOP THE CLOCK AND KEYBOARD
010000          LD     BC,0           ;SCANS. FOR BC=0 TO -65536
DBFE     LOOP   IN     A,(0FEH)       ;LET A=IN(254)
0F              RRCA                  ;LET A=INT(A/4)
0F              RRCA
D3FE            OUT    (0FEH),A       ;OUT(254),A(SPEAKER 'ON')
AF              XOR    A              ;LET A=0
D3FE            OUT    (0FEH),A       ;OUT(254),A(SPEAKER 'OFF')
10F5            DJNZ   LOOP           ;NEXT BC
0D              DEC    C
20F2            JR     NZ,LOOP
3E7F            LD     A,7FH          ;TEST FOR BREAK KEY.
DBFE            IN     A,(0FEH)       ;IF NOT PRESSED THEN REPEAT
1F              RRA                   ;THE SEQUENCE.
38EB            JR     C,LOOP
FB              EI                    ;TURN THE CLOCK AND KEYBOARD
C9              RET                   ;SCANS BACK ON, RETURN TO
                END                   ;BASIC.
```

No POKEs are needed for this routine; to begin "listening" just
use the line

                LET L = USR (start address of routine)

Start the tape player (Preferably with a tape in) and
"boogie-on-down" to the merry old sound of Glen Miller (or
whatever takes your fancy). To stop the routine, press the
BREAK key (on its own, or with any other key) and the machine
will come back into BASIC. Remember that if the routine was
called from a BASIC program then the program itself will only
normally stop if you press CAPS SHIFT as well as BREAK. The
BREAK key is only checked once every second or so, therefore

the computer will not always respond instantly when you press
the key: hold it down until the return to BASIC has ocurred.

An interesting offshoot of this program is that every time the
EAR socket is read part of the keyboard is also read. The
values obtained from this are sent out through port 254, which
apart from controlling the speaker also controls the BORDER
colour of the TV screen. You will find that by pressing certain
keys you can vary the BORDER colour (or shade, for the benefit
of the non-coloured reader!).

It works like this:

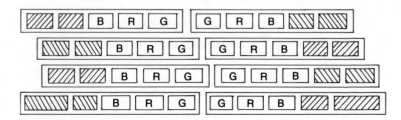

The keyboard can be considered as being split up into eight
'half-rows', each of five keys. The three keys in each half-row
that are nearest to the centre of the keyboard correspond to
the three primary colours Green, Red and Blue, and these three
colours used in various combinations produce all the other
colours of the Spectrum (sorry!).

When a key is pressed the corresponding primary colour is
removed from the 'palette' or border, leaving the resulting
combination of the other two colours. Hence depressing a Red
key leaves green and blue, which together make cyan. Note that
when all three colours are removed (by pressing three keys)
then black (or "total absence of colour") results, while
depressing no keys leaves all three primary colours, thereby
producing white.

CHAPTER 33
SPEECH REPRODUCTION

Following on from the 'Tape Relay' routine in the last chapter,
I hereby reproduce a pair of routines that will let you store
and reproduce speech on your Spectrum. No extra hardware is
required.

The process works by taking the signal sent to the EAR socket
on the Spectrum by your tape player, and turning it into a
succession of 1s and 0s. These are then stored in groups of
eight as bytes in the memory. When the sound is needed again
these bytes are taken from the memory in the same sequence in
which they were stored, broken back down to 1s and 0s and sent
to the speaker (pun unavoidable). The resulting sound should be
a good approximation of what was on the tape cassette.

Due to the high 'sampling rate' (the frequency at which the EAR
socket is 'read') needed to produce intelligible speech, large
amounts of memory are needed to store the shortest of words.
Typically this equates to a memory consumption of 1 - 2K of RAM
per second of sound.

For this reason, although it is perfectly feasible to store
speech on the 16K machine, you will have to restrict yourself
to two or three words in order to have room for a decent-sized
BASIC program.

Before proceeding further on how to use the routines, I'll give
you the pleasure of typing them in — don't forget to SAVE them
when you've finished!

```
HEX.            ;LISTEN    LENGTH : 78 BYTES
                START   EQU     5AFFH
                LIMIT   EQU     4000H
                DELAY   EQU     0CH
                ;
21FF5A                  LD      HL,START        ;SOUND IS STORED
110040                  LD      DE,LIMIT        ;DOWNWARDS FROM
E5                      PUSH    HL              ;START AND NOT
A7                      AND     A               ;EXCEEDING LIMIT IN
ED52                    SBC     HL,DE           ;MEMORY
23                      INC     HL
4C                      LD      C,H             ;BC HOLDS COUNT OF
45                      LD      B,L             ;SPARE BYTES REMAIN-
E1                      POP     HL              ;ING IN LO-HI ORDER
383A                    JR      C,END2
0C                      INC     C
F3                      DI                      ;DISABLE INTERRUPTS
167F                    LD      D,7FH           ;D IS USED IN BOTH
D9                      EXX                     ;REGISTER SETS FOR
1680                    LD      D,80H           ;SPEED AS A CONSTANT
D9                      EXX
3E7F            WAIT    LD      A,7FH           ;TEST BREAK KEY
DBFE                    IN      A,(0FEH)        ;AND RETURN TO BASIC
1F                      RRA                     ;IF HIT
302B                    JR      NC,END2
CB6F                    BIT     5,A             ;WAIT UNTIL A SOUND
20F5                    JR      NZ,WAIT         ;IS DETECTED
D9              NXTBYTE EXX                     ;LOOP FOR EACH BYTE
5A                      LD      E,D
DBFE            NXTBIT  IN      A,(0FEH)        ;READ THE EAR SOCKET
CB17                    RL      A               ;STORE THE RESULTING
CB17                    RL      A               ;BIT IN THE E REGISTER
CB1B                    RR      E
3806                    JR      C,NODELAY       ;HAVE A TIMING DELAY
060C                    LD      B,DELAY         ;UNLESS ON THE 8TH BIT
10FE            SELF    DJNZ    SELF
18F0                    JR      NXTBIT          ;REPEAT FOR EACH BIT
7B              NODELAY LD      A,E
D9                      EXX
77                      LD      (HL),A          ;STORE THE FINISHED
2B                      DEC     HL              ;BYTE IN MEMORY
7A                      LD      A,D             ;TEST BREAK KEY
DBFE                    IN      A,(0FEH)        ;IF HIT THEN RETURN
1F                      RRA                     ;TO BASIC OTHERWISE
3005                    JR      NC,END          ;CONTINUE UNTIL ALL
10E2                    DJNZ    NXTBYTE         ;RESERVED MEMORY IS
0D                      DEC     C               ;USED UP
20DF                    JR      NZ,NXTBYTE
23              END     INC     HL              ;NOW TO CONSERVE
7E                      LD      A,(HL)          ;MEMORY BACKTRACK
3C                      INC     A               ;THE POINTER TO THE
28FB                    JR      Z,END           ;LAST DETECTABLE SOUND
2B                      DEC     HL
44              END2    LD      B,H             ;RETURN THE ADDRESS
```

```
4D                      LD      C,L         ;OF THE NEXT FREE
FB                      EI                  ;BYTE TO BASIC
C9                      RET
                        END
```

HEX.   ;SPEAK   LENGTH : 69 BYTES

```
              START   EQU     5AFFH
              ENDD    EQU     4000H
              DELAY   EQU     0CH
              ;
21FF5A                LD      HL,START    ;START AND END
110040                LD      DE,ENDD     ;ADDRESSES OF SOUND
E5                    PUSH    HL          ;IN MEMORY
A7                    AND     A
ED52                  SBC     HL,DE
23                    INC     HL          ;BC HOLDS COUNT OF
4C                    LD      C,H         ;BYTES OF SPEECH
45                    LD      B,L         ;REMAINING IN LO-HI
E1                    POP     HL          ;ORDER
0C                    INC     C
3A485C                LD      A,(5C48H)   ;STORE THE BORDER
0F                    RRCA                ;COLOUR IN THE ALTERNATIVE
0F                    RRCA                ;C REGISTER
0F                    RRCA
E607                  AND     7
D9                    EXX
4F                    LD      C,A
E5                    PUSH    HL          ;H' HOLDS CONSTANT
2610                  LD      H,10H       ;10H USED AS A MASK
D9                    EXX                 ;LATER
F3                    DI
7E          NXTBYTE   LD      A,(HL)      ;TAKE A BYTE OF SPEECH
0F                    RRCA
0F                    RRCA
0F                    RRCA
0F                    RRCA
D9                    EXX
5F                    LD      E,A
1608                  LD      D,8         ;FOR 8 BITS
7B          NXTBIT    LD      A,E         ;STORE THE BIT IN BIT
A4                    AND     H           ;4 OF A, PUT THE BORDER
B1                    OR      C           ;COLOUR IN BITS 0-2 AND
D3FE                  OUT     (0FEH),A    ;OUTPUT THE BYTE ON
CB0B                  RRC     E           ;PORT 254
15                    DEC     D           ;HAVE A TIMING DELAY
2806                  JR      Z,NODELAY   ;UNLESS THE 8TH BIT
060C                  LD      B,DELAY
10FE        SELF      DJNZ    SELF
18F0                  JR      NXTBIT      ;NEXTBIT
D9          NODELAY   EXX
2B                    DEC     HL          ;LD A,00 IS A 7,T-STATE
3E00                  LD      A,00        ;TIMING EQUALIZER WITH
10E1                  DJNZ    NXTBYTE     ;THE LISTEN ROUTINE
0D                    DEC     C
20DE                  JR      NZ,NXTBYTE
```

```
D9          END     EXX
E1                  POP     HL          ;RETRIEVE HL' TO AVOID
D9                  EXX                 ;A CRASH ON RETURNING
FB                  EI                  ;TO BASIC
C9                  RET
                    END
```

Before any speech can be stored you must reserve some RAM for
it and tell the routines where that space is. We do this by
lowering RAMTOP with the CLEAR instruction. RAMTOP will already
be lower than usual since room was needed for the routines
themselves.

We define the two ends of the area reserved for speech with the
aid of the two variables, START and LIMIT. The sound is stored
DOWNWARDS in memory, so START is the highest free bytes and
LIMIT is the lowest. For example, let's suppose that the LISTEN
routine is stored at 65290 (on a 48K machine) and SPEAK starts
at 65221. Now assuming you haven't any other routines above
RAMTOP, we can let START = 65220 (one less than SPEAK).
Reservering, say, 20K of memory, we let

$$LIMIT = 65220 - (20 * 1024) + 1$$
$$= 44741$$

and to reserve this space we must reduce RAMTOP to one less
than the LIMIT, i.e.

CLEAR 44740

To use the parameters START and LIMIT in the LISTEN routine, we
use a by now familiar looking set of POKEs. If LIS is the start
of the routine,

POKE LIS + 1, START - 256 * INT(START / 256)
POKE LIS + 2, INT(START / 256)
POKE LIS + 4, LIMIT - 256 * INT(LIMIT / 256)
POKE LIS + 5, INT(LIMIT / 256)

In a similar way, we must define the START and END addresses
of the speech to be replayed by the SPEAK routine. START will
always be greater than or equal to END, and is the same value
as that used in the LISTEN routine.
When the LISTEN routine is used, it returns the value of the
next free byte below the speech just stored. As a result we
can find END by using the command

LET END = (USR LIS) + 1

to call the LISTEN routine.

To set the START and END parameters of the routine with start
address SPK,

POKE SPK + 1, START - 256 * INT(START / 256)
·POKE SPK + 2, INT(START / 256)

```
              POKE SPK + 4, END - 256 * INT(END / 256)
              POKE SPK + 5, INT(END / 256)
```

The rate at which the LISTEN routine reads the EAR socket is
controlled by the 'timing delay' in the central loop of the
routine. This controls the length of time between samples, so
the higher the delay value, the lower the sampling rate and
the poorer the speech. There is an identical delay loop in the
SPEAK routine, and I have carefully matched all other loops of
the two routines so that given the same delay values, there
will be no change of pitch between the input and output sound.
The delay value ranges from 1 to 256, with 0 corresponding to
256. I find that values up to about 45 can produce intelligible
speech, but this is largely a matter of personal preference. I
have set the standard value as twelve, since I use this most
often. To alter the delay value

```
              POKE LIS + 48, [Delay value]
              POKE SPK + 50, [Delay value]
```

It is worth bearing in mind that as the delay value decreases,
the memory will be used up faster. In fact at a delay value of
one the sampling rate is about 50 KHz (fifty thousand times per
second) and the memory is used up at about 6K per second.

Now for the practicalities of using the routines. Any signal to
the EAR socket will do as long as it is strong enough. I find
the best signal using stardard equipment is produces as
follows:

1) Insert a blank tape into the cassette player.

2) Set the recorder going in 'RECORD' mode, having first
disconnected the MIC connection to the Spectrum.

3) Speak loudly and clearly into the microphone. You may need
to shout, but if the recording is distorted then you are too close
to the microphone. The aim is to get as 'loud' a signal as
possible, without distortion.

4) Having made the recording, and leaving the MIC lead
disconnected, connect the EAR socket of the tape recorder and
the Spectrum.

5) Set the volume to maximum and the tone control (if you have
one) to maximum treble. These levels are rough guides; you may
need to experiment.

The LISTEN routine is what is known as "voice-activated", that
is to say that once called with the USR function it will wait
until it detects a signal on the EAR port before beginning to
eat its way through your spare RAM. The routine will stop
automatically when it reaches the LIMIT of RAM, but if you want
to stop it beforehand (to prevent unwanted sound being stored,
say) then just press the BREAK key. In either case, the routine

will 'backtrack' up the memory until the last detected sound is
found (said the poet who didn't know it) and return you the
address below it, so as not to waste memory storing silence.

At the end of this chapter I have included a fully operational
program that will let you build up and manipulate a vocabulary
of speech, but for the impatient I have also included a short
demonstration program. I have preset the standard values of
START, LIMIT and END to cover the complete display and
attribute files. Together these are 6 3/4K long, and so form an
adequate and somewhat spectacular temporary store for speech.

Here is the program; don't forget to alter the start addresses
to suit.

```
10 REM SPEECH REPRODUCTION DEM
O
20 REM START ADDRESSES
30 LET LIS=65290: LET SPK=6522
1
40 RANDOMIZE USR LIS: BORDER 2
50 RANDOMIZE USR SPK
60 PAUSE 30: GO TO 50
```

Having prepared your speech sample as previously described, set
the player running and RUN the program. All being well, the
screen will fill up with seemingly ramdom colours and
patterns, then the border will turn red and the Spectrum will
begin to speak. If nothing happens at all, then you have either
made an error in entering the routines, in which case the
machine has probably crashed, or the input level at the EAR
socket is too low. Press BREAK and make a fresh sample in the
latter case, shouting more loudly into the microphone.

It is worth mentioning at this point that pre-recorded
cassettes will do just as well, as long as they are loud
enough. Something else you might like to try is 'replaying' the
16K ROM by setting the START and END parameters of SPEAK to
16383 and 0 respectively, and then using the direct command:

                RANDOMIZE USR SPK

I come now to one of the largest BASIC programs in this book,
"Spectrum Speech". The program takes the effort out of using
the routines by handling all the POKEs and calculation of the
START, END and LIMIT parameters for you. While providing all
the basic functions that I feel are necessary I have kept the
program fairly concise in order to leave plenty of spare RAM
for 16K users, hence the lack of a 'menu' and other frills.

Line 30 of the programs CLEARS RAMTOP to reserve storage area
for the spoeech. I have arbitrarily chosen 32767 for RAMTOP;
this reserves about 32K of RAM on a 48K machine. 16K owners
will find that by omitting all the REM statements RAMTOP can be

lowered to about 27000. That gives almost 5.5K of speech storage. You should set LIMIT in line 90 to one more than the value CLEARED, and START in line 80 one less than the lower of the start addresses LIS and SPK in lines 50 and 60, which should also be adjusted. Don't forget to leave room (by lowering START) for any other routines you may want to use.

The command RUN will clear all the variables and set up the system to build a vocabulary of speech (lines 100 to 200). You can view the contents of this vocabulary with the direct command GOTO 210 (not RUN 210, as this would clear the variables). The START and END addresses of each word along with the timing delay used will be shown. You should note these down, since you will need them to use the SPEAK routine in your own programs (by POKEing them back into the routine).

Any of the words on its own can be heard with the command GOTO 280, and the entry can be changed with GOTO 320. The central subroutines used by the program are lines 370 to 510 (LISTEN) and lines 520 to 590 (SPEAK).

It is there that all the POKEing is done.

Lines 600 and 610 are optional and simply used in conjuction with SAVE ... LINE 600 to make the program auto-run.

GOTO 620 lets you save any or all of the speech. You will be provided with the start address of the block of code; this should be noted down. When you come to reload this speech from your own program you should use the lines:

                    CLEAR [start address] - 1
                    LOAD "" CODE

in that order.

Array A() is used to hold three peices of data for each entry. The first is the delay value and a great deal of pleasure can be derived from altering it, thereby raising or lowering the pitch of your voice. The second entry is the value of START and the third is the value of END for that word.

I'll end with a summary of commands and this listing itself.

Command	Effect
RUN	Build a vocabulary
GOTO 210	View the vocabulary
GOTO 280	Hear any word
GOTO 320	Change any word
GOTO 620	SAVE speech
LET A(W,1) = K	Alter delay value of word W

```
10 REM SPECTRUM SPEECH
20 REM © DAVID M. WEBB, 1983

30 CLEAR 32767: REM MEMORY RES
ERVED
40 REM ROUTINE START ADDRESSES

50 LET LIS=65000
60 LET SPK=64900
70 LET ZE=SIN PI: LET ON=SGN P
I: LET TW=ON+ON: LET TH=INT PI:
LET PO=256: REM CONSTANTS
80 LET START=64899: REM FIRST
FREE BYTE
90 LET LIMIT=32768: REM LAST F
REE BYTE
100 REM BUILD A VOCABULARY ****

110 INPUT "Maximum no. of words
:";M: IF M<ON THEN  GO TO 110
120 INPUT "Maximum word length:
";N: IF N<ZE THEN  GO TO 120
130 DIM A(M,TH): DIM N$(M,N): R
EM (A) HOLDS DELAY & START & END
 ADDRESS OF EACH WORD, (N$) HOLD
S WORD NAMES
140 FOR C=ON TO M: REM  C COUNT
S WORDS
150 INPUT "Please give word ";(
C);":";A$
160 LET N$(C)=A$( TO (LEN A$ AN
D LEN A$<=N)+(N AND LEN A$>N))
170 GO SUB 370: REM LISTEN
180 IF A(C,TH)=LIMIT THEN  PRIN
T "Out of memory": STOP
190 NEXT C
200 PRINT "VOCABULARY COMPLETE"
: STOP
210 REM *** VIEW VOCABULARY****

220 CLS : PRINT "NO. WORD";TAB
15;"DELAY";TAB 21;"START";TAB 28
;"END"''
230 FOR C=ON TO M
240 PRINT C;TAB TH;N$(C);TAB 18
;A(C,ON);TAB 21;A(C,TW);TAB 27;A
(C,TH)
250 GO SUB 520: REM SPEAK
260 NEXT C
270 STOP
280 REM **** HEAR ANY WORD*****

290 INPUT "Which of the ";(M);"
 words do you want"'"to hear?";C
```

```
 300 IF C>M OR C<ON THEN  GO TO
290
 310 GO SUB 520: STOP
 320 REM *** CHANGE ANY WORD ***

 330 INPUT "Which of the ";(M);"
 words do"'"you want to change?"
;C
 340 IF C>M OR C<ON THEN  GO TO
330
 350 LET START=A(C,TW): LET LIMI
T=A(C,TH)
 360 GO SUB 370: STOP
 370 REM ****** LISTEN *********

 380 POKE LIS+ON,START-PO*INT (S
TART/PO)
 390 POKE LIS+TW,INT (START/PO)
 400 POKE LIS+4,LIMIT-PO*INT (LI
MIT/PO)
 410 POKE LIS+5,INT (LIMIT/PO)
 420 INPUT "Timing delay (1-255)
:";D
 430 POKE LIS+48,D
 440 LET A(C,ON)=D: LET A(C,TW)=
START
 450 INPUT "Press ENTER to begin
 listening"; LINE a$
 460 CLS : PRINT "Press BREAK or
 just wait to end listening"
 470 LET A(C,TH)=(USR LIS)+ON
 480 IF A(C,TH)>START THEN  PRIN
T "No sound detected": LET C=C-O
N: RETURN
 490 GO SUB 520
 500 LET START=A(C,TH)-ON
 510 RETURN
 520 REM ******* SPEAK *********

 530 POKE SPK+ON,A(C,TW)-PO*INT
(A(C,TW)/PO)
 540 POKE SPK+TW,INT (A(C,TW)/PO
)
 550 POKE SPK+4,A(C,TH)-PO*INT (
A(C,TH)/PO)
 560 POKE SPK+5,INT (A(C,TH)/PO)
 570 POKE SPK+50,A(C,ON)
 580 LET A=USR SPK
 590 RETURN
 600 REM OPTIONAL AUTO-LOAD SECT
ION **************************

 610 CLEAR 64899: LOAD "LISTEN"C
ODE 65000: LOAD "SPEAK"CODE 6490
0: RUN
```

```
620 REM ***** SAVE SPEECH *****

630 INPUT "SAVE from word no. "
;C1'"to word no. ";C2
640 IF C1>M OR C2>M OR C1<ZE OR
C2<ZE OR C1>C2 THEN  GO TO 630
650 LET ST=A(C2,TH): LET LE=A(C
1,TW)-ST+ON
660 IF LE<ZE THEN  PRINT "NEGAT
IVE LENGTH": GO TO 630
670 CLS : PRINT "WRITE THIS DOW
N!"'"START ADDRESS=";ST
680 INPUT "FILENAME:";A$
690 IF A$="" OR LEN A$>10 THEN
GO TO 680
700 SAVE A$CODE ST,LE
```

CHAPTER 34
MULTICOLOURED BORDER

This following routine will produce for your visual delight a multi-coloured BORDER around your text. You thought it was impossible? Certainly not, indeed it can even be done in BASIC.

At this point may I ask readers with a 60 Hz mains supply (including North Americans) to read the values in brackets. Inside your computer is a very powerful chip which goes by the mysterious name of U.L.A. (Uncommitted Logic Array) which is responsible amongst other things for handling the television output from the Spectrum.

Inside a colour T.V. are three (or one in the case of a black and white set) electron guns, each responsible for one of the primary colours blue, red and green. In order to build up one "frame" of the television picture, the three beams move in unison from left to right of the screen at high speed, gradually moving down the screen and producing one very thin "scan line" for every horizontal sweep. Coated on the screen in an orderly fashion are three different types of phosphor, each emitting one of the three primary colours when the electron beam hits it. The lines of phosphor are so close together that their colours can mix to produce all the other colours that the eye sees, each colour being produced in accordance with the T.V. signal which effectively decides which of the electron beams are to be "switched on" for each point on the scan line.

All of the above operation is carried out at very high speed, since it takes just one fiftieth (sixtieth) of a second for the guns to build up each frame of the T.V., including the period

during which the beam is in "flyback" from the bottom of the
screen to the top.

Now the T.V. signal that I just mentioned is generated by the
U.L.A., which reads the output port 254 in order to determine
which colour to send out to the T.V. whenever the beam is
producing the border. We can show this by way of the command

OUT 254, n

where n is the required border colour. The change of border is
only temporary, since whenever the BASIC operating system
detects a key-press it changes the colour according to the
contents of location 23624.
Incidentally, the effect of BORDER n is simply to output the
new value to port 254 and adjust location 23624.

The interrupts which scan the keyboard and update the real time
clock occur 50 (60) times per second, exactly the same
frequency as the T.V. frame-production, and also exactly in
phase with the high-point of the beam's path.

We can use this identical frequency to synchronise border
colour changes by way of the PAUSE 1 command, which has the
effect of "wait for an interrupt". Immediately after this we
can have as many border-colour changes as time will allow in
the fiftieth (sixtieth) of a second before the next interrupt.
If the program has not come back to the PAUSE by this time then
severe flashing will occur since the port 254 will not then
have the same value in it every time the television scan comes
to any fixed point. Assuming that the program does get back to
a PAUSE within a fiftieth (sixtieth) of a second, the effect
will be a number of stationary coloured bands on the border,
one for each BORDER change. This program will demonstrate how
to produce a BASIC multi-coloured border; if you have a 60 Hz
mains supply then you may need to remove one of the BORDER
commands in line 30.

```
  10 REM BASIC MULTIBORDER
  20 GO TO 40
  30 PAUSE 1: BORDER 1: BORDER 2
: BORDER 3: BORDER 4: BORDER 5:
BORDER 6: BORDER 7: BORDER 0: BO
RDER 1: BORDER 2: GO TO 30
  40 BORDER 2: CLS
  50 FOR a=1 TO 8: READ B,C
  60 FOR d=1 TO b: PRINT  PAPER
C,,
  70 NEXT d: NEXT a
  80 PRINT #0;AT 0,0; PAPER 1,,
  90 GO TO 30
 100 DATA 1,2,3,3,4,4,3,5,3,6,3,
7,3,0,2,1
```

You may find that you cannot see the first stripe, which should be blue, or that it is thinner than the others. This is because immediately after the PAUSE the T.V. beam is still in "flyback" from the last frame, and it takes a millisecond or two before the beam comes down to the top of the screen.

As you can see from the program, the maximum number of stripes obtainable from BASIC is ten. this number decreases if you locate line 30 further down a BASIC listing, since in order to execute the GOTO at the end of the line the BASIC interpreter has to scan through the listing from the beginning until it finds the line. Obviously the further down the listing the line is, the longer it takes for the interpreter to find it and the less time there is to execute BORDER commands.

Incidentally, this serves as a good illustration of the fact that if you put any subroutines at or near the beginning of a program instead of at the end then the program will take less time to execute its GOSUBs and will run that much faster.

I come now to a machine-coded multi-coloured border, which as you would expect, is far more versatile than the BASIC one. You can have as many horizontal stripes as you like, and it is interesting to note that with more than 625 (525) stripes (the no. of T.V. scan lines per frame,) you are bound to get a change in colour along each scan line as well as between lines!

In order to use the routine, it is best to start with the line

LET X = (start address)

The range of colour values for the stripes is decided as follows:

POKE X + 6, (first colour's value)
POKE X + 5, (last colour's value)

Both values are inclusive and can be found by reading the number on the key below the appropriately coloured legend on the top row of the keyboard. The routine works in modulo eight, so if we want the sequence of stripes "yellow, white, black, blue" (6, 7, 0, 1), then:

POKE X + 6, 6: POKE X + 5, 1

The routine works like a PAUSE and could indeed be used as a colourful substitute in programs: it will either wait a fixed number of T.V. frames or stop when a key is pressed, whichever happens first. To define the length of the "pause", P,

POKE X + 1, P - 256 * INT (P/256)
POKE X + 2, INT (P/256)

omitting the last command if P is less than 256. Finally we have the two interlinked parameters of the number of border-changes per frame, and the length of time between

changes (the depth of the stripe). Obviously the deeper the
stripes the fewer you can fit on the screen.

As a general guide, the product of the depth and no. of stripes
should not exceed a constant value, found from this table:

	Max. (stripes x depth)	Mains Supply 50 Hz	60 Hz
Location of routine in RAM	Bottom 16K	1920	1600
	Top 32K	2400	2000

Aha! I hear you cry, the value for a 16K machine is lower
than for a 48K machine where the routine has been placed in the
top 32K of memory. Allow me to explain.

The bottom 16K of RAM is located physically on eight 16K-bit
memory chips, one for each of the eight bits that go to make up
a byte. Hence any "reading" or "writing" to the bottom 16K of
RAM involves accessing all of these chips. Now the memory that
is used to store the screen is in this 16K, and 345600 (414720)
times per second the ULA must "read" a byte from the screen
memory in order to produce the display. Only one chip can have
access to the RAM chips at any one instant, and since the
U.L.A.'s job is time dependent and involves the incredibly
accurate timing needed to produce a steady picture, it takes
priority over the humble Z-80A micro-processor which is "brought
to a halt" until it can use the RAM.
The Z-80A has to continually read the RAM chips in order to
find out what its next instruction is, and for this reason
machine-code placed in the lower 16K of RAM runs about 20%
slower than identical code placed in the top 32K of a 48K
machine, which the U.L.A. doesn't use.

Anyway, back to the script; to specify the number of stripes,
N,

        POKE X + 37, N - 256 * INT (N/256)
        POKE X + 38, INT (N/256)

and to specify the depth of the stripe, D

        POKE X + 52, D - 256 * INT (D/256)
        POKE X + 53, INT (D/256)

As it stands, this routine produces for five (4 1/6) seconds 20
stripes with depth 80 and colours 3-6 (magenta to yellow) and
so should work without flashing on any of the four memory/power
supply combinations. Here it is, along with a demonstration
program.

```
HEX.          ;MULTICOLORED BORDER  LENGTH: 68 BYTES
21FA00   START      LD    HL,00FAH      ;PAUSE LENGTH.
E5                  PUSH  HL
110603              LD    DE,0306H      ;D=FIRST COLOUR, E=LAST
7B                  LD    A,E           ;COLOUR.
3C                  INC   A
E607                AND   7
5F                  LD    E,A
E1       WAIT       POP   HL
AF                  XOR   A             ;TEST FOR A KEY-PRESS
DBFE                IN    A,(0FEH)      ;(INCLUDES EITHER OF THE
2F                  CPL                 ;SHIFT KEYS).
E61F                AND   1FH           ;IF A KEY IS PRESSED
2004                JR    NZ,STOP       ;THEN PREPARE TO STOP.
7C                  LD    A,H           ;IF THE PAUSE COUNT IS
B5                  OR    L             ;ZERO THEN PREPARE TO STOP.
2009                JR    NZ,NXFRAME
3A485C   STOP       LD    A,(5C48H)     ;TAKE NORMAL BORDER COLOUR
0F                  RRCA                ;FROM SYSTEM VARIABLE
0F                  RRCA                ;BORDER.
0F                  RRCA
D3FE                OUT   (0FEH),A      ;OUT 254,COLOUR.
C9                  RET                 ;RETURN TO BASIC.
2B       NXFRAME DEC    HL             ;DECREMENT PAUSE COUNTER.
E5                  PUSH  HL
211400              LD    HL,0014H      ;HL=NUMBER OF STRIPES.
76                  HALT                ;WAIT FOR AN INTERRUPT.
7A       NXTSEQ  LD    A,D             ;A HOLDS THE BORDER COLOUR.
08       NXTCOL  EX    AF,AF'          ;IF WE'VE PRODUCED THE
7C                  LD    A,H           ;LAST STRIPE THEN GO BACK
B5                  OR    L             ;TO SCAN KEYBOARD AND
28DE                JR    Z,WAIT        ;WAIT FOR AN INTERRUPT.
2B                  DEC   HL
08                  EX    AF,AF'
D3FE                OUT   (0FEH),A      ;CHANGE THE BORDER COLOUR.
08                  EX    AF,AF'
015000              LD    BC,0050H      ;A SHORT DELAY LETS A
78       DELAY   LD    A,B             ;STRIPE BE PRODUCED.
B1                  OR    C
0B                  DEC   BC
20FB                JR    NZ,DELAY
08                  EX    AF,AF'
3C                  INC   A             ;INCREMENT COLOUR COUNT. IF
E607                AND   7             ;WE'VE JUST USED THE LAST
BB                  CP    E             ;COLOUR THEN REPEAT THE
20E7                JR    NZ,NXTCOL     ;SEQUENCE, OTHERWISE NEXT
18E4                JR    NXTSEQ        ;BORDER COLOUR.
                    END
```

The table I gave you previously where the product of depth and
no. of stripes should reach a constant in order to fill the
screen is usually good enough for low numbers of stripes, but
for higher values we must use a more accurate formula, as

incorporated in the demonstration program. Now we have that, to avoid flashing,

$$0 \leqslant = \text{stripes} \times (117.5 + 26 \times \text{depth}) \leqslant = (\text{a constant})$$

That constant is given by the table following:

Location of routine in RAM		Mains Supply	
		50 Hz	60 Hz
	Bottom 16K	54800	45666
	Top 32K	65800	57083

Hence for a given number of stripes, N, and a constant K, to fill the screen,

$$\text{DEPTH} = (K/N - 117.5)/26$$

Note that depth should always be non-negative, so a line

IF SGN DEPTH = -1 THEN LET DEPTH = 0

should be incorporated, as in line 110 of the demonstration, if there is any chance of depth being negative.

Remember to adjust the start address in line 40 and the constant K in line 50. I have included lines 200 onwards as an example of one way to save and load the program and routine together.

```
10 REM MULTICOLORED BORDER
20 REM DEMONSTRATION
30 REM © DAVID M. WEBB 1983
40 LET MULTI=65368-68: REM STA
RT ADDRESS
50 LET K=68500: REM CONSTANT F
OUND FROM TABLE BELOW. THIS IS F
OR A 48K MACHINE ON A 50HZ SUPPL
Y
60 POKE MULTI+1,0: POKE MULTI+
2,2: REM PAUSE LENGTH
70 POKE MULTI+6,1: REM BLUE IS
 FIRST COLOR
80 POKE MULTI+5,0: REM BLACK I
S LAST COLOR
85 PRINT AT 10,2;"THERE ARE NO
W";TAB 22;"STRIPES."
90 FOR A=0 TO 9
100 LET STRIPES=2+A: PRINT AT 1
0,17;STRIPES
```

```
  110 LET DEPTH=(K/STRIPES-117.5)
/26: IF SGN DEPTH=-1 THEN  LET D
EPTH=0: REM NOTE THE NEW DEPTH F
ORMULA
  120 LET HI=INT (STRIPES/256)
  130 POKE MULTI+37,STRIPES-256*H
I
  140 POKE MULTI+38,HI
  150 LET HI=INT (DEPTH/256)
  160 POKE MULTI+52,DEPTH-256*HI
  170 POKE MULTI+53,HI
  180 RANDOMIZE USR MULTI
  190 NEXT A: GO TO 9999
  200 REM I USED THIS TO LOAD THE
  ROUTINE FROM TAPE....
  210 CLEAR 65367-68: LOAD "MULTI
BORD"CODE 65368-68: RUN : REM 65
367 WAS RAMTOP
  220 REM ...AND THIS TO SAVE THI
S PROGRAM,WHICH AUTOLOADS THE RO
UTINE
  230 SAVE "MB DEMO" LINE 200: SA
VE "MULTIBORD"CODE 65368-68,68
```

CHAPTER 35
SOUND EFFECTS

The only sound effect available to you on a standard Spectrum is the BEEP command, so I thought one of the most useful inclusions in this book would be a versatile set of sound routines to enhance your programs.

There are three routines in this chapter, and for technical reasons they each sound different when placed above or at address 32768 to when placed below that address.

The reason for this is that the ULA chip (the one that produces the T.V. picture) and the Z-80 (the one that runs machine code) both need access to the memory chips that hold addresses up to 32767, and since the ULA has priority and only one chip can use the memory at any one time, the Z-80 has to wait until the ULA has finished. This "waiting" on the part of the Z-80 results in a rougher tone and a longer average delay between the "clicks" that produce the note, causing a lower pitch. Above address 32767, the note will be purer and have a higher pitch.

If you have a 16K machine, then the routine will always be below address 32768 (you have no RAM above that address). If, however, you have a 48K machine, then the routine will normally be above address 32767, and you will get a purer tone. In order to try the rougher note (which in my opinion often sounds better), you'll need to CLEAR "RAMTOP" below 32768. To do this use the direct command:

CLEAR 32767.

Now RUN the Hexaid program, and use option one to enter the routine in the normal manner. The cost of this technique is that you only have as much room left for a BASIC program as you would on a 16K machine, so bear this in mind when using it.

The first routine produces a short "whooping" sound, and if called repeatedly in a short BASIC loop produces a very effective warning siren. No POKEs are required.

```
HEX.       ;SIREN  LENGTH: 21 BYTES
3A485C    START   LD    A,(5C48H)      ;TAKE BORDER COLOUR.
0F                RRCA
0F                RRCA
0F                RRCA
1E00              LD    E,0
F3                DI                    ;DISABLE INTERRUPTS.
D3FE      NXCLICK OUT   (0FEH),A        ;CLICK.
EE10              XOR   10H
43                LD    B,E
10FE      SELF    DJNZ  SELF            ;DELAY.
1D                DEC   E               ;INCREASE PITCH UNTIL
20F6              JR    NZ,NXCLICK      ;MAXIMUM,....
FB                EI                    ;THEN ENABLE INTERRUPTS
C9                RET                   ;AND RETURN TO BASIC.
                  END
```

You can increase the pitch that the note starts off at (and hence shorten the sound) with a simple POKE. If "S" is the start address, then

POKE S + 7, [new value]

That "new value" is in the range 0 to 255, where 1 is the highest pitch, decreasing towards 255 and finally to 0, which can be thought of as 256, the lowest pitch and the value in the standard routine.

The second routine works in the exact opposite direction to SIREN and sounds like a space-age "laser shot" above address 32767, or a Winchester "rifle-shot" below it. Again, if "S" is the start address, then you can decrease the pitch that the note starts off at (shortening the sound) with the command.

POKE S + 7, [new value]

Where the new value is as described for SIREN.

```
HEX.       ;LASER SHOT LENGTH: 21 BYTES
3A485C    START    LD    A,(5C48H)      ;TAKE BORDER COLOUR.
0F                 RRCA
0F                 RRCA
0F                 RRCA
1E01               LD    E,1
F3                 DI                   ;DISABLE INTERRUPTS.
D3FE      NXTCLIK  OUT   (0FEH),A       ;CLICK.
EE10               XOR   10H
```

```
43                  LD    B,E
10FE      SELF      DJNZ  SELF          ;DELAY
1C                  INC   E             ;DECREASE PITCH
20F6                JR    NZ,NXTCLIK    ;UNTIL MINIMUM
FB                  EI                  ;THEN ENABLE INTERRUPTS.
C9                  RET                 ;RETURN TO BASIC
                    END
```

The next routine is a WHITE NOISE generator. That is to say
that it produces a series of clicks in quick succession but at
varying and fairly random lengths of time apart. The resulting
sound is a sound like an explosion or static picked up on a
radio.

For the mathematicians among you, I have written a
pseudo-random number generator producing a cyclical sequence
of 256 numbers containing each integer in the range 0 to 255.
Taking the Fermat prime 257 (= 2 to the power of 8 + 1) and
one of its primitive roots, 254, the residue of

$$(254)^i \text{ modulo } 257 \qquad (0 <= i <= 255)$$

minus one is the sequence of 256 distinct numbers used. This
can be illustrated with a simple BASIC program that generates
the sequence:

```
10 REM PSUEDO-RANDOM GENERATOR
15 REM @ DAVID M. WEBB 1983
20 LET P=257: LET A=254
25 REM P IS PRIME, A IS THE PR
IMITIVE ROOT MODULO P
30 LET SEED=A↑0
40 FOR R=1 TO 256: PRINT R,SEE
D-1
50 LET SEED=A*SEED: LET SEED=S
EED-P*INT (SEED/P): REM SEED=(SE
ED*A)MOD P
60 NEXT R
```

The pseudo-random number generator is used in the routine to
produce the delay between clicks.

To use the routine, the only parameter needed is the duration
of the sound. Let this be "D", and the start address be "W".
Then

```
POKE W + 12, INT(D / 256) :
POKE W + 11, D - 256 * INT(D / 256)
```

specifies the duration, the standard value of which is 128.
Here is the routine, followed by some tips on how to get the
most out of it, and a demonstration program.

```
HEX.            ;WHITE NOISE  LENGTH: 48 BYTES
F3        START    DI                      ;DISABLE INTERRUPTS.
3A485C             LD      A,(5C48H)        ;TAKE BORDER COLOUR.
0F                 RRCA
0F                 RRCA
0F                 RRCA
08                 EX      AF,AF'           ;H HOLDS (SEED-1)
2600               LD      H,0
018000             LD      BC,0080H         ;BC HOLDS DURATION.
08        NXTCLIC  EX      AF,AF'           ;CLICK.
D3FE               OUT     (0FEH),A
EE10               XOR     10H
08                 EX      AF,AF'
2E00               LD      L,0              ;LET HL=256*(SEED-1)
55                 LD      D,L
5C                 LD      E,H
A7                 AND     A
ED52               SBC     HL,DE            ;LET HL=HL-2*(SEED-1), SO
ED52               SBC     HL,DE            ;HL=254*SEED-254.
11FE00             LD      DE,254           ;LET HL=HL+254, SO
19                 ADD     HL,DE            ;HL=254*SEED
7D                 LD      A,L              ;LET H=HL MODULO 257
94                 SUB     H
3801               JR      C,HOP
3D                 DEC     A
67        HOP      LD      H,A              ;STORE NEW SEED IN H
3D        SELF     DEC     A                ;DELAY LOOP.
20FD               JR      NZ,SELF
0B                 DEC     BC               ;REPEAT FOR DURATION
78                 LD      A,B              ;OF SOUND.
B1                 OR      C
20DF               JR      NZ,NXTCLIC
FB                 EI                       ;ENABLE INTERRUPTS.
C9                 RET                      ;RETURN TO BASIC.
                   END
```

Varying effects can be produced by altering the duration of the
noise and then calling the routine within a short BASIC loop.
Values of about 64 to 200 can sound like a machine gun, as
shown by this program:

```
   10 LET NOISE=65000: REM INSERT
 YOUR OWN START ADDRESS
   20 INPUT "DURATION ";D
   30 POKE NOISE+11,D-256*INT (D/
256)
   40 POKE NOISE+12,INT (D/256)
   50 IF INKEY$<>"" THEN  RANDOMI
ZE USR NOISE
   60 GO TO 50
```

You can use the program to experiment with other durations, holding down a key to hear their repeated effect. A value of 2 sounds like a light aircraft in level flight; a value of about 10 is like a motorbike cruising on open roads; a value of 200-260 sounds like the starting motor on a car. Higher values can be used for explosions.

Obviously we cannot hope to exactly duplicate the real-life sounds described above, but you will probably find that the use of text or graphics illustrating the source of the simulated sound adds to the realism of the effect (e.g. animating an aeroplane whilst simulating its engine noise). This demonstration program will show you what I mean: don't forget to alter the start address of the routine in line 30!

```
10 REM WHITE NOISE DEMO
20 REM © DAVID M. WEBB 1983
30 LET NOISE=65000: REM START
ADDRESS
40 POKE NOISE+11,220: POKE NOI
SE+12,0: REM DELAY OF 220
50 PRINT "A DAY IN THE LIFE OF
 A CAR......";AT 10,12;"START!!!
"
60 FOR A=0 TO 3
70 FOR B=0 TO 7+5*RND
80 PAUSE 2: RANDOMIZE USR NOIS
E
90 NEXT B
100 IF A<>3 THEN  PAUSE 25+50*R
ND
110 NEXT A
120 PRINT AT 10,12;"BROOOM"
130 POKE NOISE+11,2: REM LENGTH
OF 2
140 FOR A=0 TO 400: RANDOMIZE U
SR NOISE: NEXT A
150 POKE NOISE+11,0: POKE NOISE
+12,12: REM LENGTH OF 2560
160 PRINT AT 10,12;"SMASH!!!"
170 RANDOMIZE USR NOISE
180 STOP
190 SAVE "NOISE DEMO" LINE 210:
SAVE "NOISE"CODE 65000,48
200 STOP
210 CLEAR 64999: LOAD ""CODE 65
000: RUN
```

CHAPTER 36
PRINTER CONTROL USING OUT

You may have seen mentioned on page 160 of the Spectrum manual
that the printer is addressed by port 251. I will elaborate on
this.

Your ZX printer can run at three speeds; fast, slow and zero.
The stylus which burns away the aluminium coating to reveal
the black backing of the paper can either be on or off. The
speed and stylus status can be controlled by OUT-putting a
number to port 251. The output port is 'latched', that is to
say that once a value is output it remains there until the next
one is sent. For example, if you turn the printer motor on it
will stay on until the value to turn it off is sent, whatever
the Spectrum happens to be doing in the meantime.

The command to operate the printer is
                OUT 251,N

and here are the values of N and their effects.

It is probably not a good idea to leave the stylus on for too
long, or overheating may result.

VALUE Of N	EFFECTS
128	Motor fast, Stylus on.
0	Motor fast, Stylus off.
130	Motor slow, Stylus on.
2	Motor slow, Stylus off.
4	STOP

I have included a little subroutine which can be used as a
computer-controlled line feed.


```
9000 REM KEYBOARD PRINTER LINE-F
EED CONTROL SUBROUTINE
9010 REM PRESS AND HOLD DOWN L F
 OR LINE-FEED, X TO ESCAPE
9020 IF INKEY$="X" OR INKEY$="x"
 THEN  RETURN
9030 IF INKEY$="L" OR INKEY$="l"
 THEN  OUT 251,0: GO TO 9020
9040 OUT 251,4: GO TO 9020
```

APPENDIX A
A LIST OF ROUTINES WITH PAGE AND LENGTH

APPENDIX B
USING THIS BOOK WITH THE MICRODRIVE

Information on the Microdrive became available at too late a date for inclusion in the main text of this book, so here it is.

Although the increase in speed when saving short blocks of machine code is negligible, the Microdrive does have the advantage of taking less time to find the code when loading it back than for tape.
The Hexaid Program in chapter one is easily altered to SAVE and LOAD machine code on a Microdrive cartridge by making the following changes:

Where K is the Microdrive number.

```
615 PRINT "Insert cartridge and hit any Key":
    PAUSE 0
620 SAVE * "m"; K; n$ CODE A, VAL A$
Delete line 660
670 VERIFY * "m"; K; n$ CODE
790 PRINT "Insert cartridge and hit any Key":
    PAUSE 0
800 LOAD * "m"; K; n$ CODE VAL A$ :GO TO 680
```

The SPECTRUM SPEECH program in chapter 33 can be altered to SAVE speech on Microdrive K with the line

```
700 SAVE * "m"; K; A$ CODE ST,LE
```

Using a Microdrive to store the speech will speed things up considerably, due to the massive length of such blocks.
I would like to draw your attention to the list of system variables for coping with the Microdrive, Network and RS 232 Interface on page 47 of the ZX Interface 1 and ZX Microdrive manual. In particular, you can change the colour assumed by the border during input and output to the interface by the command:

```
POKE 23750,(colour number(0-7)).
```

APPENDIX C
FURTHER READING

In this book I have refrained from attempting to teach the
reader how to program in machine language, but have instead, I
hope, shown the vast increase in speed and power over BASIC
that such an ability can offer. I have endeavoured to include
all the routines a Basic programmer is ever likely to need for
program enhancement, but if you would like to take the next
logical step and begin writing YOUR OWN machine code then I
would recommend the Melbourne House book, "Spectrum Machine
Language For The Absolute Beginner".

The book takes you gently through the elementary ideas behind
machine language and on to a thorough working knowledge of it,
culminating in the step-by-step development of a fully -
fledged machine code arcade game.

While the above-mentioned book adopts an informal approach to
machine language with special reference to a particular
computer, if you want a more clinical and technical approach to
programming the Z-80 in general then
Rodnay Zaks' "Programming The Z-80" is to be recommended.

Be warned, however; it can be rather heavy going for the
beginner and is more appropriate as a reference aid to a fluent
machine language programmer.

Also of interest to the reader who wants to know what makes the
Spectrum tick (or should I say "buzz") is "Understanding Your
Spectrum" by my colleague Dr Ian Logan and published by
Melbourne House. This book explains concisely the rudiments of
machine language and goes on to delve into the 16K Rom and
reveal some very useful details on how the 'operating system'
works, and how to use it to your advantage.

*　　　*　　　*　　　*

NOTES

NOTES

NOTES

NOTES

SUPERCHARGE YOUR SPECTRUM

REGISTRATION CARD

Please fill out this page and return it promptly in order that we may keep you informed of new software and special offers that arise. Simply cut along the dotted line and return it to the correct address selected from those overleaf.

Where did you learn of this product?

☐ Magazine. If so, which one? . . . .

☐ Through a friend.

☐ Saw it in a Retail Store

☐ Other. Please specify . . . .

Which Magazines do you purchase?

Regularly: . . . .

Occassionally: . . . .

What age are you?

☐ 10-15   ☐ 16-19   ☐ 20-24   ☐ Over 25

We are continually writing new material and would appreciate receiving your comments on our product.

How would you rate this book?

☐ Excellent   ☐ Value for money
☐ Good   ☐ Priced right
☐ Poor   ☐ Overpriced

Please tell us what software you would like to see produced for your SPECTRUM.

_____

_____

_____

Name _____

Address_____

_____ Code _____

PUT THIS IN A STAMPED ENVELOPE AND SEND TO:
In the United States of America return page to:
Melbourne House Software Inc., 347 Reedwood Drive, Nashville TN 37217.

In the United Kingdom return page to:
Melbourne House (Publishers) Ltd., Melbourne House, Church Yard, Tring, Hertfordshire, HP23 5LU

In Australia & New Zealand return page to:
Melbourne House (Australia) Pty. Ltd., Suite 4, 75 Palmerston Crescent, South Melbourne, Victoria, 3205.